PATHWISE® Data-Driven
School Improvement Series

CONCEPTUALIZING
A NEW PATH

Peter J. Holly

Teaching and Learning Division

Educational Testing Service
MS 18-D
Rosedale Road
Princeton, NJ 08541-0001
Web site: http://www.ets.org/pathwise

Copyright © 2003 by Educational Testing Service (ETS). All rights reserved.

Educational Testing Service, ETS, the ETS logo, Pathwise and the Pathwise logo are registered trademarks of Educational Testing Service.

No part of this publication may be reproduced or transmitted in any form or by any means, electronic or mechanical, including photocopy, recording, or any information storage and retrieval system, without permission from ETS.

ISBN 0-88685-243-9

Printed in the United States of America

07 06 05 04 03 02   10 9 8 7 6 5 4 3 2 1

Table of Contents

Introduction v
Purpose of Workbook One v
Group Process Guide vii
Structuring Learning Team Meetings xiv

Chapter One: The Problem of Change 1
The Purpose of Chapter One 1
The Change Wars 1
    Task 1: Alternatives to Change Wars 2
    Task 2: Personal Experiences with Change Wars 3
    Task 3: District Initiatives 7
    Task 4: Categorizing Reactions to Change 14
    Task 5: Setting Change to Music 15
    Task 6: Reflecting on Chapter One 18

Chapter Two: The Seven Elements of School Improvement 21
The Purpose of Chapter Two 21
Element One: Getting Focused 23
    Task 1: Applying Focusing Skills 24
    Task 2: Recognizing the Developmental Stages of Change 30
    Task 3: Planning and Sequencing Changes Over Time 31
    Task 4: Clustering Changes 33
    Task 5: How to Say "No" 34
Element Two: Creating a Shared Agenda 37
    Task 1: Instant Gardening 37
    Task 2: Relating the Six Factors for a Healthy Life to Professional Situations 41
    Task 3: Creating a Central List of Common Ground Issues 43
    Task 4: Listening to Others' Views and Opinions 45
    Task 5: Rating Your School's Current Approach to Change 49
Element Three: Follow-Through — Sustaining Changes Over Time 51
    Task 1: Changing Trains — A Metaphor 51
    Task 2: Sustaining Changes Over Time 53
    Task 3: Reflecting on Element Three 59
Element Four: Grounding Our Change Efforts in Data 61
    Task 1: Action Planning 67
    Task 2: Understanding the Interests of Stakeholder Groups ... 70
    Task 3: Tracking Student Progress 73
Element Five: Data Show Our Progress 75

Task 1: Understanding the Role of Data in School Improvement Efforts 75
Task 2: Creating Your Local Version of Essential Learnings 80
Task 3: Constructing a Needs Assessment Tool 82
Task 4: Identifying Local Keepers of the Vision 84
Task 5: Completing a Gap Analysis 85
Task 6: Reflecting on De-Centering 88

Element Six: Continuous Improvement in the Self-Renewing School 91
Task 1: Applying the Characteristics of a Learning School 92
Task 2: Identifying Local External Requirements and Internal Needs 94
Task 3: Attending to Both External Requirements and Internal Needs 95
Task 4: Using the Properties of a Self-Renewing School to Complete
         a Local Assessment 98
Task 5: Evaluating the Performance of Your School System 100
Task 6: Understanding the Difference Between Site-Based and
         Shared Decision Making 105
Task 7: Integrating School-Based Initiatives with System Coordination 107
Task 8: Constructing a Decision-Making Matrix 109
Task 9: Reviewing the Guidelines for Making Good Decisions 111
Task 10: Composing a Common Public Agreement 112
Task 11: Understanding the Impact of Voting in the Decision-Making Process . .113
Task 12: Filtering Change 114

Element Seven: Creating a Data-Driven School Culture 117
Task 1: Identifying Strengths and Challenges 117
Task 2: Summarizing Survey Findings 121
Task 3: Reflecting on Local Efforts in Light of Dubuque Schools' Efforts 123
Task 4: Reflecting on Data Coach Training 127
Task 5: Finding Time to Learn From Data 129
Task 6: Reflecting on Your School Culture 130
Task 7: Identifying an Effective Leadership Style 133
Task 8: Rating the Effectiveness of the Site Council 136
Task 9: Developing an Action Plan 138
Task 10: Sharing New Ideas with Colleagues 140
Task 11: Reflecting on New Learning 141

About the Author 144
References 145
Appendix 149

INTRODUCTION

This workbook is for educators who wish to commit to data-based decision making for continuous school improvement. It is the first of several related workbooks and, as such, provides an overview for the entire series—PATHWISE® *Data-Driven School Improvement*. While the companion volumes will cover different aspects of data-based decision making, this first workbook presents the fundamental argument that data-based decision making constitutes a valid, alternative method of going about educational change. Indeed, the author argues that the ways in which we have been encouraged to change previously have actually hindered—even incapacitated—us as change makers and have left an indelible, negative imprint on the collective psyche of educators. Data use and shared decision making are not ends in themselves; they are the connected means to ends that really matter—school improvement for enhanced student achievement. How this is all done constitutes a new and more educator-friendly way of generating change in education. What is also different about this workbook is that it is both an invitation to participate in the change process and, in terms of the practical exercises and tasks included, an ongoing set of supports for those who accept the invitation. The series of workbooks is designed for Learning Teams and Study Groups ("Change Circles") with opportunities for individual reflection built into the collaborative process. However, each workbook can also be useful for individual educators, who would then be encouraged to share their reflective work with immediate colleagues, and for a whole school faculty, working in small groups and coming together to share ideas and make decisions.

Other workbooks in this series will cover such related topics as follows:

- data-driven school improvement
- data processing
- classroom action research
- leadership for continuous improvement

PURPOSE OF WORKBOOK ONE

The central purpose of this workbook is to orient educators to an alternative way of going about change in schools and school districts. Change is constantly in demand. Indeed, whereas change is the constant, it is the way we go about change that is the variable. In order to deal with the constancy of change demands, new attitudes, skills, and knowledge about an alternative path for the processing of change are required. It is the purpose of this workbook to generate all three: new attitudes toward the change process, new knowledge about this alternative path and why it is necessary, and capacity building in terms of skill acquisition.

In his speeches, the author, Peter Holly, talks about the need to be proactive and approach change with a clenched fist and not the separated fingers of a splayed hand. The significance of the clenched fist metaphor is that it represents an approach that is much more likely to have power in its punch; it is a metaphor that reappears in several different ways throughout this workbook. It speaks, for instance, to the model itself—data-based decision making for continuous improvement in schools. This is a tightly packaged, integrated, well-honed cluster of innovations (see Guskey, 1990). Other commentators besides Holly have called for similar configurations (Bernhardt, 1998, Love, 2000, Holcomb, 1999) and have linked data-based decision making to school improvement. In Holly's approach, however, they become one—with each constituent part virtually disappearing in the mix.

This is a timely effort for two reasons. Firstly, demands for change are not going away. Indeed, recent legislation at the national level on both sides of the Atlantic has added to the volume of demands. Typically, however, the swelling demands for change are not accompanied by proportionate increases in the system's capacity to deal with the changes. The one always seems to outstrip the other. This workbook series constitutes a real attempt to rectify this imbalance. Secondly, there is mounting evidence that if multiple changes are attempted without concomitant moves on the process side of the equation, two negative factors can impinge crucially on the change situation. One is that harried, over-burdened instructors teach less effectively and, as a result, their students fare less well in terms of their learning—the very antithesis of the aims of school improvement.

School improvement done badly, therefore, can defeat the central purpose of school improvement: the advancement of student learning. The other is that teachers are so inundated with having to make "content" and "technical" changes in their individual classrooms that the kind of collaborative school climate that comes with the activation of staff collegiality is the first casualty—just at a time when, more than ever, teachers need the support, encouragement, and positive reinforcement of their colleagues. This workbook aims to ward off both these dangers.

This is why the tasks and activities contained in this workbook are so integral to its purpose. By tackling the exercises, both individually and cooperatively, participants acquire the skills and attitudes to become not only better change makers but also better colleagues and more effective team players. As Calhoun (2002) asserts, the kind of approach advocated in this workbook can have instructional *and* social benefits. By doing collaboration skillfully, teachers become yet more collaborative—which, in turn, positively influences the climate of their school. The quality of data-based, *shared* decision making is crucially dependent on the quality of the collaborative process that underpins it—thus the importance of the following **Group Process Guide** that has been prepared for the effective use of this workbook.

GROUP PROCESS GUIDE

The PATHWISE: *Data-Driven School Improvement Series* is a set of tools designed to assist teams of teachers and administrators in the process of school improvement. Although an individual wishing to improve the teaching and learning in a single classroom could undertake many of the activities, the activities are generally presented in the context of group work. The workbooks are sequential in moving through the school improvement process, and the activities are sequential within each workbook. Each activity is designed to build upon those that precede it and to add to the groundwork for those that follow. This **Group Process Guide** is provided to assist facilitators and team members in making the activities effective in achieving their intended purposes. In some instances the activities are intended to help teams identify areas for school improvement focus; other activities are meant to help the team members hone their skills in the group process.

The completion of activities by a school improvement team should reflect the style and needs of that unique team. For a variety of reasons, different teams will move through the tasks with different time requirements and differing levels of commitment to the specific tasks. Some teams who use the materials may be coming together for the first time; others may be long existing and well functioning prior to using these materials as a guide in the school improvement process. It is important to allow your team to use the activities provided to assist your work, but allow your own style to influence how you accomplish each task.

Stages of Group Development

A brief discussion of the stages of groups may assist teams in identifying their level of development. When a team first begins its work together, it is in the **Forming** stage. At this stage the leader/facilitator must take a strong role as the group is still dependent on the leader for guidance and direction. The team's questions focus on the clarity of the task. The behavior of the team is usually polite, impersonal, and sometimes, guarded. Scott Peck (1987), in his discussion of the stages of community making, has labeled this stage "pseudocommunity." He issues a caution for groups in this stage—there is a tendency to fake it by avoiding any conflict and "being extremely pleasant with one another" (p. 86). School improvement teams should use this polite phase to agree on the task at hand and the ground rules that will guide their work as each task inevitably becomes more challenging.

School teams who are grappling with difficult school improvement issues will, quite naturally, move to the next stage of development—**Storming**. This stage also requires the skill of an effective facilitator along with group process techniques to move effectively through the stage. Peck (1987) aptly calls this stage "chaos" as the inevitable conflicts among members become apparent. Part of the storming aspect of this stage can be attributed to the tendency of team members to attempt to convert others to their way of thinking. A challenge for the facilitator and team members in this stage is to be aware that confrontations in this stage tend to be confronting people, rather than issues. The ground rules agreed in the **Forming** stage become useful and necessary at this stage. The chaos that the team feels at this stage is not counterproductive; confronting the differing ideas in the group increases the understanding of each other among the team members. It also allows them to examine the strength that each differing opinion brings to their team's effectiveness.

It is this understanding of their diversity that assists groups in moving to the third stage—**Norming**. As individual team members come to feel understood by the others and come to appreciate the strengths in their colleagues, they are able to "empty" (Peck, 1987) the need to convert others to their way and replace that need with a commitment to finding the collective good for the school. During the **Norming** stage, groups are developing the skill to make group decisions. Procedures for group work become routine and expected. The team is able to give and receive feedback and to confront issues rather than individuals. For many teams, this phase happens so quickly and easily, in comparison to the **Storming** phase, that they find themselves in the fourth stage without recognizing the third.

Stage Four is **Performing**—or "community" in Scott Peck's (1987) terms. At this point the team has matured into a closeness; they are "in community" with one another. Teams that have achieved this level of effectiveness are resourceful, flexible, open, and supportive. They are able to accomplish difficult tasks and make challenging decisions. They share ideas and strategies while respecting the gifts of other team members.

The purpose of including this overview of group development in this **Group Process Guide** is twofold. First, it is important that teams understand that *all* groups go through these stages of development to get to the point where they can function most effectively and efficiently. Groups should, therefore, anticipate these stages and not be surprised by the group experiences in each stage. Second, there is a caution about Stage Two—**Storming**. Because *all* groups must go through these stages, the storming cannot be avoided if a team truly desires to become a "performing" team. It is possible to retreat back into the politeness of pseudocommunity, but the team will not function as well or achieve as much if the members are unwilling to do the hard work of becoming a high-functioning team.

Group Process Techniques

Ground Rules

Facilitators and team members can take advantage of a variety of group process techniques to assist them in moving through their development and thereby, ensure that they accomplish their intended purpose—to improve their schools. Most of these strategies and techniques are like the paddles of a war canoe and used only when appropriate and necessary. However, the foundation for all strategies, and therefore necessary at all times, are GROUND RULES (sometimes referred to as norms or group behavior expectations). Examples of ground rules are as follows:

- Seek opportunities to be involved.
- Praise others, no putdowns.

- Seek to understand, then to be understood (active listening).
- Include all members (a community feeling).
- Empathize—put yourself in another's place.
- Offer the right to pass.
- Ensure confidentiality—what is said in the group, stays in the group.

Groups should establish the ground rules that enable them to work together respectfully in all phases of development. It is the ground rules that assist a group in working through the storming phase while maintaining the integrity of the group's work.

Strategies

As stated above, the following group process strategies will be selected and implemented depending on the activity to be accomplished. The following list of strategies and activities, while an attempt to be comprehensive, is not exclusive. Facilitators and team members are encouraged to use other strategies that they have found to be effective in the school improvement planning process. There are excellent resource materials available that provide further ideas (see, in particular, Johnson and Johnson, 2000, and Garmston and Wellman, 1999). The strategies included below, however, are the ones that will be referenced and utilized in the activities in this workbook.

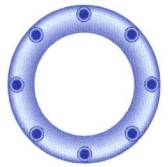

Circle Configuration

The physical arrangement for the team when working should be as close to a circle as possible. Each member of the group should be able to easily hear all others when they speak. The facilitator should sit (not stand) in the circle. All members of the team have an equal voice and equal responsibility for the success of the team.

Groupings

In order to provide team members with the opportunity to reflect and clarify their own thinking as well as to understand that of the other team members, a variety of groupings within the team should be used during activities. At times, individuals should reflect on their own. Dyads (pairs) should be used to allow all members to share their ideas in the safety of a single partnership. Triads (groups of three) can be used for the same purpose. At times it is very effective to reflect alone, then share the reflections in a dyad or triad with that subgroup coming to consensus on its position. Then dyads can be combined into quads with further clarification and consensus on issues. Groups can continue to combine with other groups until one or two larger groups have been able to find their common ground…and thus the common ground for the team.

Facilitation Skills

It is critical that all team members have the opportunity to gain facilitation skills including reflective listening, clarifying, open questioning, summarizing, encouraging, and reporting. Many teams prefer to rotate the role of the facilitator among members; other teams agree on a single facilitator for a specific period of time. Other important team roles include chairperson, process observer, recorder/reporter, critical friend, engaged participant, and, when required, translator. Garmston (2002) emphasizes that having all participants understand and agree to meeting roles is one of his five standards for successful meetings; the other four, all relevant for this **Group Process Guide**, are as follows:

- Address only one topic at a time.
- Use only one process (strategy) at a time.
- Achieve interactive and balanced participation.
- Use cognitive conflict productively.

Go Round

Research has shown that those who speak aloud in the early part of any meeting are more likely to continue to speak and share throughout the meeting. The guidelines for a Go Round are that each person in the group responds to the prompt, in turn, without interruption or comment from the other members. Go Rounds are encouraged at the beginning of each session to bring all members into the group. Go Rounds can also be used at any time to get a sense of what each member of the group is thinking — or when one or two members tend to dominate the discussion, to ensure that *all* ideas have the opportunity to be shared. Go Rounds are an excellent strategy for mobilizing the interactive and balanced participation recommended by Garmston (2002).

Team Listing

For some group activities, it is important to have one team member record each participant's ideas, suggestions, and/or opinions on poster-sized paper. This Team Listing can then be posted on the wall for easy reference and revision as needed.

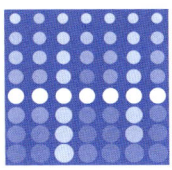
Consensus Building

It is important to define consensus. Teams sometimes create problems (perhaps an intentional block to their success) by defining consensus as everyone in complete agreement on a course of action. While an admirable goal, this is rarely achieved. A more manageable definition of consensus is that of "sufficient consensus," defined as agreement among all members of the team that they will not sabotage the implementation of a course of action that is supported by the majority, even though there may be some skepticism regarding the likelihood of its success.

There are a variety of strategies that can be used to facilitate consensus and to determine if a majority opinion exists for a course of action. A Go Round with members stating their position on a scale of 1 (low support) to 10 (high support) can be very effective. Another technique is to have each member (on a count of three) give a signal, such as "thumbs up" for support; "thumb horizontal" for ambivalence; and "thumbs down" for non-support.

There are also many published strategies for creating a consensus opinion. These are available in many books on team building, group work, and so forth, and will not be described here. Examples include cooperative processing, nominal group technique, and brainstorming.

The Tambourine

This is an excellent group processing technique that can be used to enable a group of educators to meld their individual agendas and to find common ground. The technique is called the Tambourine because it resembles a tambourine when drawn on a large sheet of poster paper. The technique works as follows: the members of the group sit in a half circle around the sheet of paper—which can be pinned to a wall or affixed to a stand. It should look like the design below.

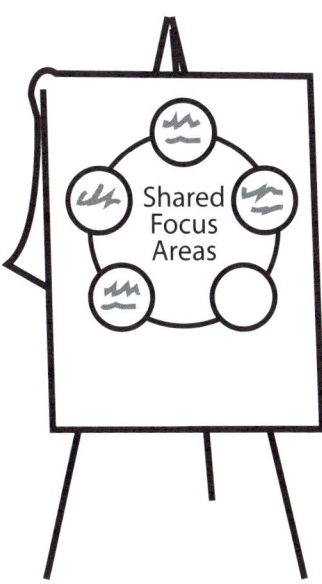

Then each individual, after careful consideration of the issues in hand, goes through his or her list of personal thoughts and ideas. The recorder/scribe writes these on the poster—within the small circle representing this particular member. This step is repeated for each individual until all the small circles are completed. Ten minutes are then devoted to silent scrutiny of what has been produced so far—with an eye to finding the "common ground" issues. Then, using a Go Round, members identify those items that are predominately in common and, if the majority of participants agree, the items are added to the inside of the larger circle—thus producing a shared agenda of common ground issues to which everyone has contributed.

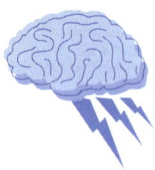

Brainstorming

During the ongoing process of school improvement, there is a recurring need for team members to generate ideas and share information. Brainstorming is an effective technique to use to solicit ideas from the group members on a given topic. When running a brainstorming session, it is important to follow these four steps: select a recorder and group facilitator; generate ideas; record the ideas; and organize the results. The brainstorming technique introduced in Workbook One is "Free-Wheel Brainstorm" where individuals are encouraged to spontaneously call out responses, remembering to abide by the following guidelines (BRAIN):

- **B**uild on each other's ideas.

- **R**efrain from judgment.

- **A**im for quantity.

- **I**magine creatively and "out of the box."

- **N**ote all suggestions.

Confronting Issues

Confronting issues is sometimes referred to as dealing with the "elephant in the living room." Groups must be willing and able to identify those things that pose barriers to their effectiveness and to openly discuss the issues and seek mutually beneficial solutions. Confronting issues will often throw a team into chaos (the Storming phase) and can seem like a setback when a team has appeared to be functioning well. However, if the stages of group processing are thought of as a spiral, each time a group cycles through the phases they emerge at a higher level on the spiral than the last time around. Although difficult and challenging, it is the act of confronting barrier issues that increases the likelihood of long-term success of any team. The GROUND RULES again become critical in helping the group discuss their problems and find solutions.

Celebrations and Closure

On an ongoing basis, groups should engage in celebrations of their accomplishments and as closure at the conclusion of their work. These celebrations should be as public as possible and should recognize the contributions of all team members. The nature of each celebration is determined by the culture of the group—from solemn, ceremonial celebrations to more party-like atmospheres.

The quality of shared decision making based on data is dependent on the quality of collaborative processes used. This Group Process Guide is intended to give teams the tools they need to develop quality group-work sessions. Teams are also encouraged to use other sources of group-processing strategies and to avail themselves of learning/training opportunities for facilitation skills if available.

STRUCTURING LEARNING TEAM MEETINGS

Before the meeting...

Adequate preparation before each team meeting by both the facilitator and team members will result in more productive team meetings. Based on the length of each team meeting, the facilitator must decide what material will be covered in the meeting and what material participants will need to cover on their own in preparation for the meeting. For example, in preparing for the first meeting to discuss Chapter One of Workbook One, the facilitator might ask team members to read on their own, prior to meeting, the sections entitled, "The Purpose of Chapter One" and "The Change Wars."

The facilitator must also decide which tasks/activities will be implemented in any given meeting. Each task in the workbook is organized as follows:

> Purpose: (Why are we doing this task?)
>
> Grouping: (How are we to work—on our own, in pairs or triads, or with the whole Learning Team?)
>
> Group process strategy: (Which strategy will most effectively support us in accomplishing the work we are doing?)
>
> Directions: (What are we doing?)

It is important for the facilitator to carefully study these four elements of a task prior to the meeting to ensure a smooth implementation of the task. Each group process strategy is explained in the **Group Process Guide**, which will serve as a handy reference throughout the use of the workbook. In addition, it is the facilitator's responsibility to ensure that any necessary materials, such as poster paper and markers, are ready for use.

During the meeting...

The group processing skills that have just been covered in the **Group Process Guide** are most frequently used in meetings. Indeed, it is in meetings that school improvement work is generally processed. For the benefit of all those concerned, such meetings need to be focused, purposeful, task-oriented, and productive. At any school improvement meeting, the basic skills and techniques of group processing need to be practiced in combination to provide for structure, flow, and, above all, task completion. In each meeting, these simple procedural rules should be utilized:

- Assign team member roles, as appropriate.
- Review the ground rules.

- Conduct a focus activity or "ice-breaker."

- Review the goal(s) of the meeting and check for understanding.

- Review any assigned reading or activity completion that occurred outside of team meetings. Provide time for both discussion and clarification as needed.

- Review the purpose of each task to be completed during the meeting and explain the group process strategy selected to accomplish the task.

- When conducting team discussions, record the key words and phrases shared, as well as any issues that might need to be revisited.

- Provide time to reflect at the end of the meeting.

- Assign reading and/or activities that team members will need to complete prior to the next meeting.

- As appropriate, provide the date and time of the next meeting, as well as a general overview of what will be accomplished.

This checklist is a very handy tool for group facilitators to use when planning school improvement meetings. Moreover, during the reflection time at the end of the meeting, it may well be advisable to invite team members to evaluate the session using the kind of review sheet found on the next page.

Team Self-Review Sheet

For each of the following statements, circle the number which best indicates your view of how your group performed, using the continuum of 1 "Strongly Disagree" to 10 "Strongly Agree."

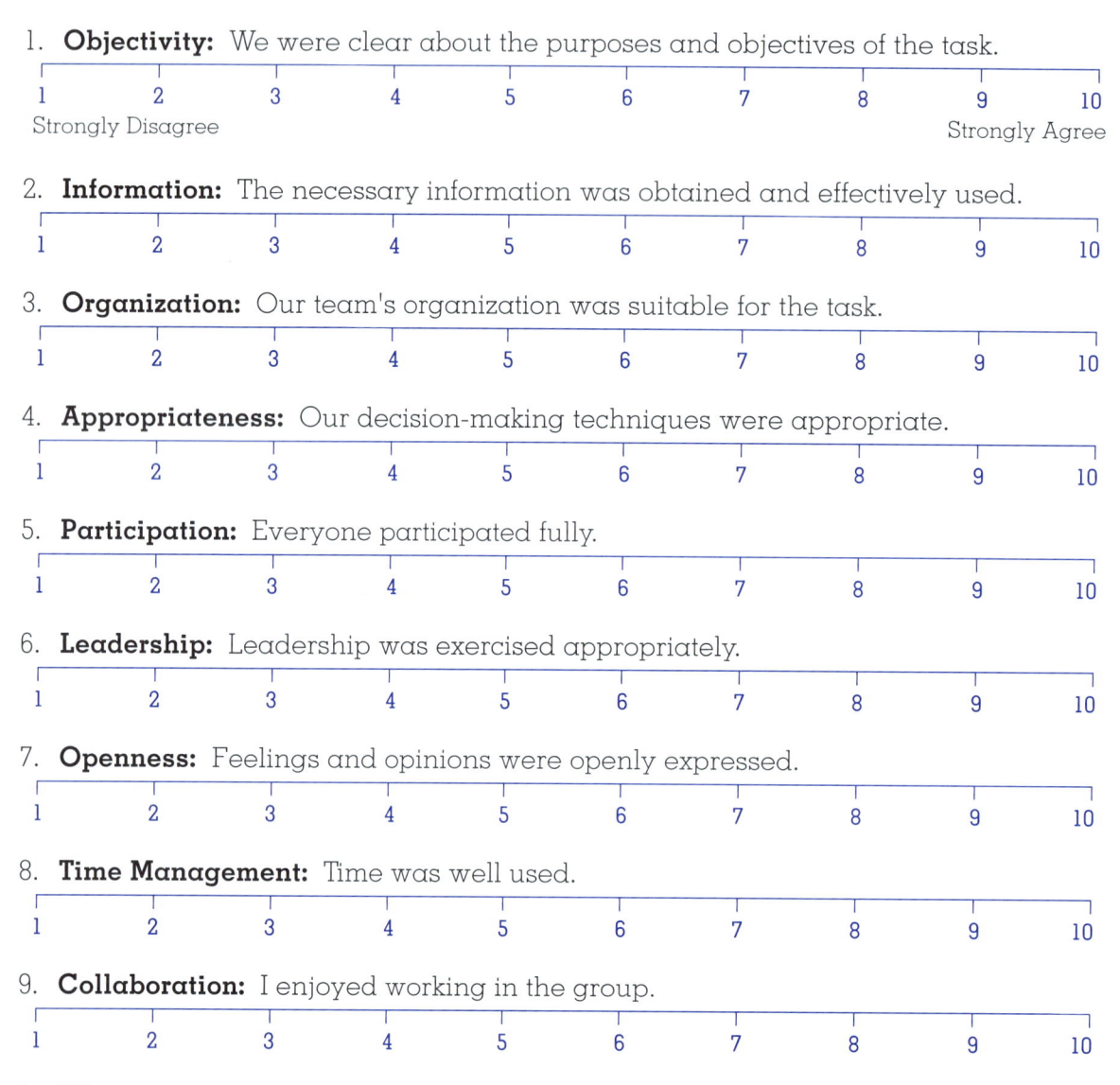

1. **Objectivity:** We were clear about the purposes and objectives of the task.

   ```
   1    2    3    4    5    6    7    8    9    10
   Strongly Disagree                    Strongly Agree
   ```

2. **Information:** The necessary information was obtained and effectively used.

   ```
   1    2    3    4    5    6    7    8    9    10
   ```

3. **Organization:** Our team's organization was suitable for the task.

   ```
   1    2    3    4    5    6    7    8    9    10
   ```

4. **Appropriateness:** Our decision-making techniques were appropriate.

   ```
   1    2    3    4    5    6    7    8    9    10
   ```

5. **Participation:** Everyone participated fully.

   ```
   1    2    3    4    5    6    7    8    9    10
   ```

6. **Leadership:** Leadership was exercised appropriately.

   ```
   1    2    3    4    5    6    7    8    9    10
   ```

7. **Openness:** Feelings and opinions were openly expressed.

   ```
   1    2    3    4    5    6    7    8    9    10
   ```

8. **Time Management:** Time was well used.

   ```
   1    2    3    4    5    6    7    8    9    10
   ```

9. **Collaboration:** I enjoyed working in the group.

   ```
   1    2    3    4    5    6    7    8    9    10
   ```

10. What might the team do differently to improve the next meeting?

CHAPTER ONE: THE PROBLEM OF CHANGE

The Purpose of Chapter One

In this chapter, the need for a new path to school improvement is established. This is accomplished by both building an in-depth critique of current change practices and creating a sense of what has to be overcome in order to be successful. In Kurt Lewin's strategy called "force-field analysis," he encourages participants to deliberate on what constrains us in attempting to go forward. It's impossible, Lewin argues, to go ahead if we don't know what we're up against. In this case, among other things, we're up against ourselves.

In this chapter, participants are encouraged to reflect on this phenomenon in the hope that they will reach the understanding that we are all part of the problem of change. As a consequence, we all have to take some of the responsibility for being part of the problem in order to become part of the solution. We have to help break the vicious cycle and self-fulfilling prophecy that educational change doesn't work—by making it work for us. By reading and using this chapter, and by engaging in awareness-raising, attitude-reforming exercises, participating team members will feel differently about change and about themselves as potential changemakers. The arguments contained in this chapter are drawn from current change theory and a great deal of field experience on the part of the author.

In 1989 this author co-authored a book called *The Developing School* in which he argued that the Developing School is the Learning School because it relies on data to learn its way forward. The messages contained in this U.K. publication met a ready audience in the United States where, for the last twelve years, he has worked with schools and districts to apply—and, in so doing, update and refine—the concepts and strategies contained in the original publication. In fact, in the process of helping schools deal with change so intensively, a viable, alternative approach to educational change making has been created. At the same time, working at ground level, he has been an observer of, and a participant in, what are now being called the Change Wars.

The Change Wars

In recent editions of Phi Delta Kappan, Robert Reys (2001) writes about the "Curricular Controversy in the Math Wars: A Battle Without Winners" and Carl Glickman (2001), writing in similar vein, entitled his article, "Dichotomizing Education: Why No One Wins and America Loses." Both authors claim that no one wins when it comes to the conflicts that occur over change in education. Reys, for example, argues that the controversy regarding standards-based mathematics curricula (as in California) continues to

CHAPTER 1

consume much energy and emotion that could be better used for more productive purposes. Differences of opinion with regard to what is important to learn and how it should be taught, he says, are nothing new in mathematics education. This time around it is the proponents of textbooks and so-called traditional programs versus the advocates of standards-based approaches.

The standards-based movement, according to Reys, represents a major change force and, as a result, has been vilified. While standards-based mathematics curricula have been accused of not being research-based, using children as guinea pigs, and not producing "the goods" when it comes to student learning results, Reys questions whether traditional programs themselves have a sterling record of success. Shouldn't all programs, he asks, be tested according to the same criteria? Glickman would definitely agree. He invites educators to jettison the "winner takes all" attitude of ideological absolutes. In such either/or debates, he says, both sides attempt to crush one another, leaving only one solution standing; each viewpoint claims to possess *the* truth, while criticizing the other. Examples cited by Glickman include: the controversy over standards; intrinsic versus extrinsic motivation; direct instruction versus constructivist learning; cooperative versus competitive learning; phonics versus whole language; and traditional versus progressive education.

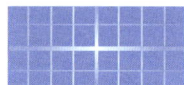
The Problem of Change
Task 1: Alternatives to Change Wars

<u>Purpose:</u> To begin to understand that the counter-productive nature of the Change Wars saps our energy, resources, and willingness to be involved in further change efforts.

<u>Grouping:</u> Meet with team members in the Circle configuration.

<u>Group process strategy:</u> Utilize the Go Round method—as described in the Group Process Guide.

<u>Directions:</u> For your team reflection, consider what might be a better approach than getting involved in these polarized and dichotomized change wars.

CHAPTER 1

 The Problem of Change ■ Task 2—Part 1: Personal Experiences with Change Wars

Purpose: To raise awareness and personal engagement—by tapping into the participants' own experiences and feelings as participants in the Change Wars.

Grouping: Work individually.

Directions: This is the first opportunity to produce personal written reflections in the spaces provided. Reflect on this quotation from Glickman's article and answer the questions that follow it.

> Many educators in classrooms and schools feel that they have become pawns in the reformers and policy makers' propaganda game that insists that there is a single best way to change the system of American schools...The 'single truth' wars have created much pain among teachers and school leaders who are swept into the battles. When whole language gained currency as *the* way to teach reading, teachers using phonics were lambasted, swept aside, and made to feel that they were evil, archaic, fascist practitioners of an indefensible method. Recently, the opposing force has 'won' in states led by California and Texas. They have blamed whole language and invented spelling for declining literacy in America. Now teachers of whole language are made to feel abandoned and rejected as 'feel-good,' self-esteem promoting contributors to the demise of basic skills (Glickman, 2001).

1. In what ways have you been caught up in similar conflicts and what were the issues involved?

CHAPTER 1

2. What happened as a result of these conflicts?

3. In being caught up in these conflicts, how did you feel? What did you think or do?

 **The Problem of Change ■ Task 2—Part 2: Personal Experiences with Change Wars**

Grouping: Work in dyad or triad groupings (see the **Group Process Guide**) and then meet with your whole group.

Directions: With your partner(s), share your answers to the questions from Part 1 and then meet as a whole group to list the experiences and feelings that you have in common using the following chart.

CHAPTER 1

	GROUP LIST: COMMON CHANGE EXPERIENCES AND FEELINGS
1.	In what ways have you been caught up in similar conflicts and what were the issues involved?
2.	What happened as a result of these conflicts?
3.	In being caught up in these conflicts, how did you feel? What did you think or do?

You are not alone...

As a result of such experiences, if you felt discouraged, frustrated, even angry, then you are not alone. Experience tells us that the seemingly endless pendulum swings involving educational fads and fashions of all kinds have left teachers feeling deeply distrusting, exhausted, and pulled and pushed in all directions—like educational marionettes. "Who is pulling our strings this time?" is a much used lament in the faculty lounge. The pendulum swings, however, are only one characteristic of the change wars. Generally, it has to be said, the change industry has not served teachers well. Typically, those charged with implementing the changes (school leaders and classroom practitioners) have no ownership in or commitment to the changes, are asked to do too much too fast, have no idea why they're working on the particular changes being sold to them, and, consequently, have no investment in following through with the changes. In 1994, for instance, the superintendent of a mid-sized district in Iowa listed in diagrammatic form all the initiatives being locally implemented (see below). The first thing to notice about this diagram is the title: District Initiatives (Not All Inclusive)—which means either that not all the changes could fit on one page or the superintendent couldn't keep track of them all! As he said to me at the time, "Help! Change is out of control here. Disregard the lines; there's no connectedness—the lines are just for artistic effect." Imagine how the teachers in that district felt.

CHAPTER 1

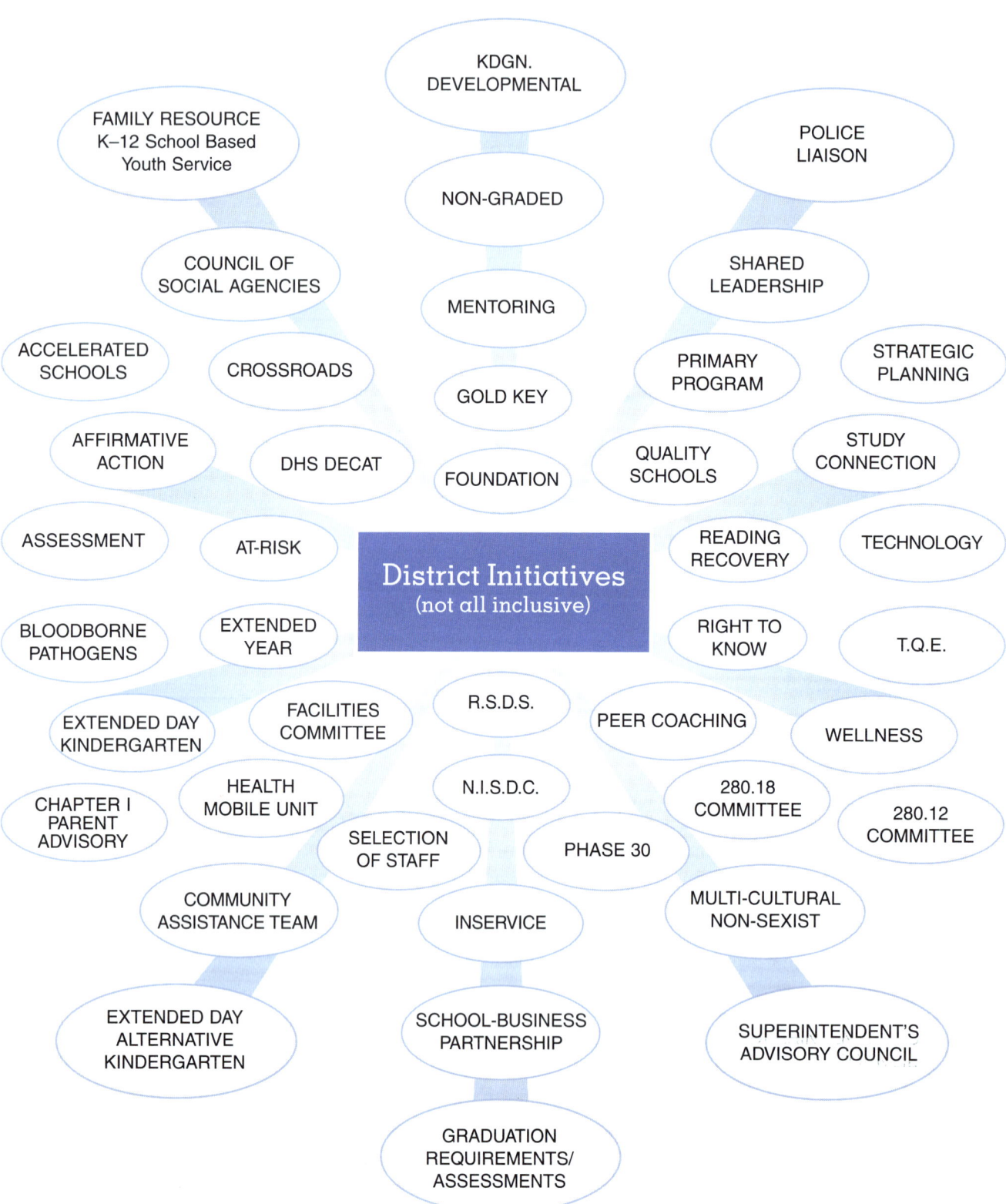

What is wrong with this picture? Actually, the diagram speaks volumes. In terms of the district's change efforts, there was neither rhyme nor reason. First, there was a complete lack of focus. What was presented was a mess of changes with no sense of some being more important than others. It's not certain that they were all current changes but they were still all lumped together. Second, as the superintendent observed, there was no connectedness. Far from it, all the various changes were in competition. Moreover, each change represented an enthusiastic interest group or committee pushing their particular pet idea.

No wonder, then, if teachers and administrators felt deluged with multiple changes. Third, there was no planning process indicated; in fact, everything (even potential change processes) was treated as content. Fourth, there was no discretion being used. There was no discernment, no filtration, and no prioritization. Above all, there was no needs identification. Which of these changes were being introduced to meet internally identified needs? Where were the data to be able to have this conversation? If there was no sifting process in place, then everything came through to the teachers—who were on the receiving end of undigested change pap. Fifth, as a result of this overload, everything remained superficial; there was no depth, no meaning, and no significance. Everything cancelled out everything else—with the end result being no change, no real implementation, definitely no institutionalization. As one group of teachers in the same district observed at the time:

> We're dancing so fast, there's no time to change...
> There's too much work for too little change.

 **The Problem of Change**
Task 3—Part 1: District Initiatives

Purpose: In this foundational task, team members will localize and begin to take ownership of the problem of change.

In working with district and school teams, the author often invites them to do their own version of what he calls the bubble diagram (or bubble map); it is called that because the picture reminds him of free-floating bubbles that will soon hit a hard surface and burst, thus dashing the hopes of those promoting them. Interestingly, the teams have usually found doing this exercise useful, enjoyable, and even cathartic. It is probably a case of not being able to make positive headway until we acknowledge the extent of our organizational unhealthiness. So now it is your turn.

Grouping: Work alone or in pairs (dyads).

Directions: Using the bubble diagram that follows, fill in all the changes with which your school and/or school district is currently wrestling. This task is also important for another reason: it is the basis for several tasks contained in the next section of this workbook.

7

CHAPTER 1

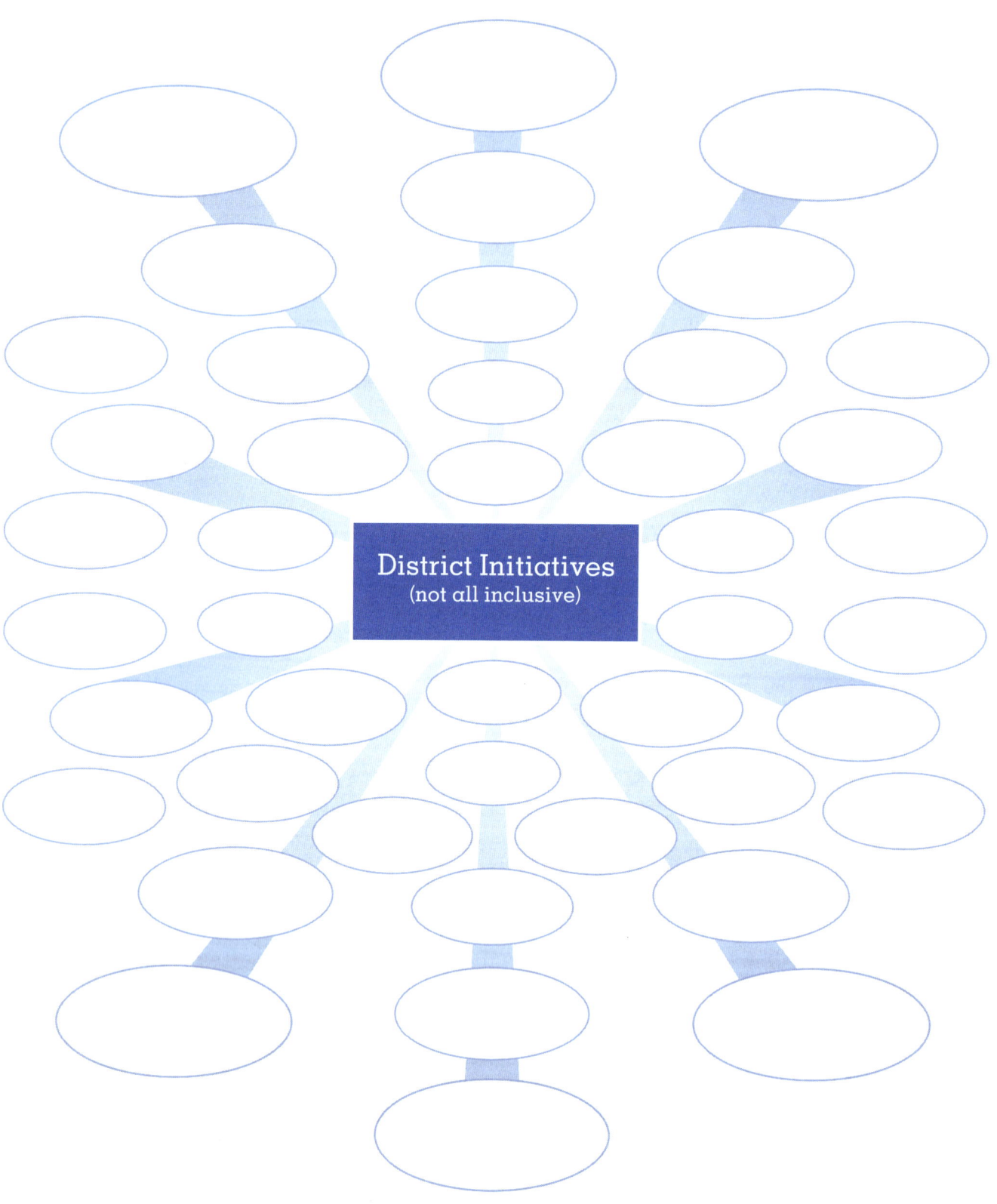

CHAPTER 1

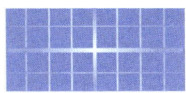
The Problem of Change
Task 3—Part 2: District Initiatives

<u>Grouping:</u> Work individually and then meet with your Learning Team.

<u>Group process strategy:</u> Use a Go Round combined with a Team Listing. Select one team member to act as the recorder.

<u>Directions:</u> Now that you have finished your local version of the bubble map, you are asked to answer the following questions about your educational change situation. Respond to the questions individually first, recording your answers below. After individual reflection, meet with your Learning Team using a basic cooperative sharing process (a combination of a Go Round followed by a Team Listing of common ground issues), with one team member acting as the recorder.

1. Looking at the finished diagram, what concerns do you have and what do you feel good about?

2. How easy was it to fill in this diagram and what does your answer tell you?

3. In your context, what contributory factors have led to the nature of your diagram?

4. Explain the relationship between what is represented on the diagram and why your change plate always seems so full.

The Effects of Change Overload and Fragmentation

Some commentators are aware of what you have experienced. In their book entitled *The Self-Renewing School*, Bruce Joyce, James Wolf, and Emily Calhoun (1993) conclude:

- School districts tend to generate multiple initiatives simultaneously and, therefore, superficially.

- The "multitude of lightly supported initiatives" gives teachers and principals a feeling of being inundated by an impossible array of demands "from above" and leaves many people frustrated at the lack of implementation. Teachers end up, they say, feeling alienated and pushed around.

- Teachers are unclear about what they are supposed to be emphasizing and how much initiative to take. Their confusion leads to cynicism, argue the same authors.

In similar fashion, Michael Fullan (1996) has argued:

> Overload and fragmentation are two major barriers to education reform, and they are related. Overload is the continuous stream of planned and unplanned changes that affect the schools. Educators must contend constantly with multiple innovations and myriad policies, and they must deal with them all at once. Overload is compounded by a host of unplanned changes and problems, including technological developments, shifting demographics, family and community complexities, economic and political pressures, and more. Fragmentation occurs when the pressures—and even the opportunities—for reform work are at cross purposes or seem disjointed and incoherent.
>
> Overload and fragmentation combine to reduce educators' motivation for working on reform. Together they make the situation that the schools face seem hopeless, and they take their toll on the most committed, who find that will alone is not sufficient to achieve or sustain reform.

CHAPTER 1

Those support agents who work with teachers on a daily basis have seen them confused and psychologically injured as casualties of the change wars and have witnessed their lack of motivation, their hopelessness, their anger, and their resentment. Educators have also been seen adopting coping strategies to prevent further injury. Thus when faculty members say, "This too shall pass; all we have to do is sit it out and it will go away like all the rest of the changes," they are using the time-honored coping strategy of not getting involved. Their thinking is, "If you don't get involved, you can't be hurt." And more often than not, they are proved right. Their experience tells them that changes do not stick around—whether they invest in them or not—so the "flavor of the month" will inevitably be relegated to next month's scrap heap. Ironically, however, by refusing to get involved (based on past experience) with current initiatives, teachers are contributing to the very phenomenon that they complain about—the transitory nature of change. When they are forced to become involved, they do so begrudgingly and half-heartedly. No wonder, then, as Elmore (1996) has pointed out, "Innovations that require large changes in the core of educational practice seldom penetrate more than a fraction of schools, and seldom last for very long when they do."

The fear, however, is that the damage to teachers as professionals goes even deeper. They are suffering from what could be referred to as institutionalized incompetence. Indeed, based on a reading of Dick Sagor's excellent book, *At-Risk Students: Reaching and Teaching Them* (1993), it is possible to be struck by the parallels between how de-professionalized teachers are feeling and how the students that Sagor refers to as discouraged learners feel about themselves. Sagor, quoting Conrath (1986), describes the most common characteristics of these students:

1. They have low self-confidence, a deeply held sense of personal impotency and helplessness, and a lack of self-worth.

2. They are avoiders. They avoid learning [change] because it is demanding and threatening. Moreover, it is confusing and unresponsive to their needs. They avoid contact with those likely to make them have to learn [change].

3. They are distrustful; teachers [change agents] have been unfair, unresponsive, even abusive.

4. They have a limited notion of the future. They do not see the future as bright or positive and tend to respond to short-run, measurable goals accompanied by demonstrations of success and competence.

5. They have good reason to be discouraged. Their experience tells them that they are behind others [their more enthusiastic colleagues], do not receive the same kind of perks, and people give up on them. "They are poisoned by a sense of intellectual incompetence."

6. They are surrounded by colleagues who feel the same way—thus compounding their feelings. Their reference group reinforces them in their despondency.

7. When they have adequate peer relationships, it is with people that they trust (i.e., people who are in the same situation).

8. They are impatient with routine and do not respond well to long-time sitting and listening. They quickly learn how to play their role as non-intellectuals and are seen as disruptive when they demonstrate their impatience, maybe by asking an intelligent question such as, "Why are we doing this?"

9. They often come from the category of learning preference identified as "practical." They remember very little of what is delivered in a linguistic style to a physically passive, note-taking audience.

10. They are externalizers—people who see the world as happening to them and one over which they have little control. They do not take personal responsibility and choose to attribute any successes that they achieve to random luck and not to any effort on their part.

This depth of disaffection and alienation is probably as common among classroom teachers as it is among at-risk students. They have been sold out one too many times (interestingly, very few commentators except Michael Fullan and Milbrey McLaughlin have questioned the "selling" paradigm of implementation) and are refusing to play the game. It's safer on the sidelines. Indeed, says Forsythe (1996), there's some good news here. Beleaguered teachers and at-risk students alike are refusing to fall into the slough of a victim mentality and are displaying resiliency in the face of adversity: they are responding negatively for positive reasons. They are resorting to the only weapon left to them—passive aggression.

Hampel (1995) has researched teacher and faculty responsiveness to change initiatives. He found four (often splintered) factions: the leaders or "vanguard" (the activists and change zealots—referred to by Joyce and Showers as the "change omnivores"); the "yes, but" people who are cautiously supportive but want to see hard evidence that this will work; the "sleepy," often soon-to-be-retired people; and the "cynics" who are bitterly resentful, who are often past innovators themselves and are still harboring past disappointments. These four groups exist in every educational establishment, but, as Hampel admits, the "yes, but" folks are by far the largest group. They tend to be the side-liners. They keep their heads down and, like all good members of the infantry, they quickly learn how to build the best foxholes. While Miller (1996) has pointed out that the "vanguard" zealots and the "cynics" have much in common (what he refers to as their present or past idealism), it is worth emphasizing the importance of winning over the "yes, but" crew—given their large numbers and their sound change philosophy of "show me it works; show me the data!"

CHAPTER 1

 **The Problem of Change**
Task 4: Categorizing Reactions to Change

<u>Purpose:</u> Those involved will appreciate how different colleagues approach changes differently.

<u>Grouping:</u> Work individually and then meet with your Learning Team.

<u>Group process strategy:</u> This is a good time to be in your Circle configuration.

<u>Directions:</u> Individually, respond with your personal reflections to the following questions. Then share your responses with the members of your Learning Team.

1. In which group would you place yourself and why?

2. In terms of your membership, what are the advantages and disadvantages of being in this particular group?

3. Have you always been a member of this group? Has your membership changed over the course of your career? Do you switch membership according to the kind of change being promoted?

CHAPTER 1

 **The Problem of Change**
Task 5: Setting Change to Music

<u>Purpose:</u> To learn together by providing fun and laughter (a cornerstone of effective group work) while making a serious point concerning the dangers of change overload.

<u>Grouping:</u> Meet with your Learning Team.

<u>Group process strategy:</u> Make a Team List and perform a skit.

<u>Directions:</u> If you need some light relief, then this is your opportunity. In your Learning Team, create a Team List of song titles (e.g., "Stop! In the Name of Love") that have some relevance to this discussion about educational change. For each title, please explain its significance. If you want to be more focused, you could just use titles of Beatles tunes (e.g., "Eight Days a Week").

When you have completed your list, plan a skit that incorporates the song titles (and maybe some actual singing!) that could be used with colleagues who are not members of your Learning Team to share some of your current thoughts about the educational change process.

So where are we?

When it comes to change, then, incapacitation is built into the educational system. The educational reform industry continues to get it wrong and teachers have come to expect it—while teachers, themselves, with their precautionary, diversionary actions, condemn many of the changes to oblivion. No one is innocent in this debacle. Commentators like Richard Elmore (1996) talk about the deep, systemic incapacity of U.S. schools. Schools, he says, are constantly changing, but not at the core; they are forced to trivialize because they lack both institutional and individual competence.

Elsewhere, Holly (2002) has referred to this same phenomenon as "lots of changes, but no changing." Elmore's conclusion is that the failure has not been on the supply side (research and knowledge generation), but on the demand side (the receiving teachers and their schools). This conclusion is somewhat questionable—for many of the reasons covered above. Indeed, Hatch (2002) has recently pointed out that program developers should accept the responsibility for helping to develop institutional capacity in schools—which may then be used to choose programs other than their own. This level of altruism, he says, can only help developers down the line—when, in turn, schools choose their programs from a position of strength involving lengthy and considered deliberation. Hatch concludes:

> It is easy to blame the principals for getting involved in too many initiatives, the districts for failing to coordinate their own initiatives, and the improvement programs for making unrealistic demands. But the problems of fragmentation and overload experienced…around the country may be a feature of an education 'system' in which schools, districts, and improvement programs face numerous, often conflicting, demands from diverse constituencies, experience frequent changes in policies and personnel, and operate with significant constraints on the time, resources, and funding available to them.
>
> As a consequence, efforts to implement and integrate different initiatives face a basic paradox: creating new incentives for improvement and aligning some policies may motivate or smooth the way for some school reform efforts, but it takes capacity to build capacity at the school level. Ironically, although improvement programs can provide some of the inspiration, resources, services, and expertise that can help schools develop capacity to change, the adoption of such programs can bring new demands, requirements, and costs that schools do not always have the capacity to meet.

Hatch's central argument is that "the cumulative demands and resulting fragmentation and incoherence can undermine the capacity of schools to make the very improvements so many desire; in other words, bad change-making experiences render those involved more incapable of making changes. Implicit in his argument is what could be called the funding trap. All schools need more resources, so they chase grant monies that, if obtained, come with strings attached—leaving the schools under-resourced. So the schools try to reduce the level of obligation—thus reducing the level of challenge and, therefore, the level of programmatic impact. Miller (1996) maintains that "blueprints for change" are developed externally, *sold* to educators who then have to turn theory into practice and, in so doing, change the changes. Drawing on the research of McLaughlin (1987) and Tyack and Tobin (1994), Miller asserts that, while reformers believe that their innovations will change schools, it is important to recognize that schools change the innovations. Over and over again, he says, teachers have selectively implemented and

CHAPTER 1

altered reforms. "Why are we surprised?" says Fullan. In his challenging article entitled, "Turning Systemic Thinking on Its Head," he states:

> **If those at the top make the mistake of thinking that reforms are 'something to be implemented', they are misunderstanding how change works, and ultimately defeat their own purpose (Fullan, 1996).**

So we are left with a basic conundrum: how to persuade educators who have been forced into what is essentially an anti-change stance to rise to the challenge of change. By using the model outlined in his original book (*The Developing School*), working "with, not on teachers" (see Lieberman, 1986) and adapting the model in the light of experience, this author has created the approaches outlined in this current workbook. He has purposefully created a model that speaks to the widest possible group of teachers—especially the "yes, but" folks.

Indeed, when speaking to teachers and administrators about the model ("School Improvement through Data-Based Decision Making"), he argues that data-based decision making helps educators to **get focused** on a **shared agenda** and to commit to **following through** with change over time. This change effort is **grounded** in rich, meaningful information that reminds the educators of the **progress** being made and the work still to be accomplished regarding **school self-renewal and continuous improvement**. The school's established infrastructure is used to create a **data-based culture** for decision making. In the next section of this workbook, each of these seven highlighted elements is covered in more detail—in terms of both commentary and practical exercises.

CHAPTER 1

 **The Problem of Change**
Task 6: Reflecting on Chapter One

<u>Purpose:</u> To reflect together and individually on the material that has been covered in Chapter One.

<u>Grouping:</u> Meet with your Learning Team.

<u>Group process strategy:</u> Use the Go Round.

<u>Directions:</u> Thinking about what you have read in this section and how you have responded to the various tasks and questions, it is now time to do two things:

- At the end of your current Learning Team meeting, for closure, do a Go Round sharing your immediate thoughts and feelings.

- Prior to your next meeting, commit to more measured reflection by completing the first entries for your personal **Change Log** that follows. The idea here—and it will happen in a recurring fashion throughout this workbook—is to commit to some reflective writing in terms of three questions:

1. What have you learned so far?

2. What are you continuing to think about?

3. What are you going to do differently in the future?

In this workbook, whenever there are **Change Log** pages for your written reflections, you will use these same three questions to guide your reflection.

CHANGE LOG
The Problem of Change

What have you learned so far?

What are you continuing to think about?

What are you going to do differently in the future?

CHANGE LOG
The Problem of Change

Notes

CHAPTER TWO: THE SEVEN ELEMENTS OF SCHOOL IMPROVEMENT

The Purpose of Chapter Two

This chapter contains extended coverage of the seven elements that constitute the new, alternative path for change making. What underpins all these elements is the use of data. Data help us understand what is essential (focus) to work on together (shared agenda) over time (follow through) as the cornerstone of continuing school improvement efforts. In addition, data provide feedback on these efforts (progress monitoring) which promotes the development of the learning organization (as a self-renewing system) that is geared for success (infrastructure). While each element has its own power, it is the synergistic power of the whole package that is significant.

These seven elements of school improvement mirror many of the broad themes of effective school leadership identified in *A Framework for School Leaders: Linking the ISLLC Standards to Practice* (Hessel and Holloway, 2002) and are aligned to the ISLLC (Interstate School Leaders Licensure Consortium) Standards. Both the elements and the ISLLC Standards focus on the ongoing improvement of student learning through the collaborative efforts of the school community.

Each element is described in some detail and the accompanying tasks are designed to foster the essential skills that contribute to the accomplishment of the element. Participants are introduced to each element and are given opportunities to note what is required, reflect on its importance, become involved in skill acquisition, commit to self-assessment, and begin to remedy identified deficiencies. The work triggered by this chapter paves the way for sustained school improvement efforts—the subject of Workbook Two. Engagement in this orientation process can only strengthen participants' future attempts to generate data-driven and continuous school improvement.

CHAPTER 2

The Elements of School Improvement

ELEMENT 1 — Getting Focused

ELEMENT 2 — Creating a Shared Agenda

ELEMENT 3 — Follow-Through—
Sustaining Changes Over Time

ELEMENT 4 — Grounding Our Change Efforts in Data

ELEMENT 5 — Data Show Our Progress

ELEMENT 6 — Continuous Improvement
in the Self-Renewing School

ELEMENT 7 — Creating a Data-Driven School Culture

ELEMENT 1

Getting Focused

Overview

Focusing has to come first. Without it there can be no positioning for success. Ries (1996) has pointed out to the business world:

> The sun is a powerful source of energy. Every hour the sun washes the earth with billions of kilowatts of energy. Yet with a hat and some sun-screen you can bathe in the light of the sun for hours at a time with few ill effects.
>
> A laser is a weak source of energy. A laser takes a few watts of energy and focuses them in a coherent stream of light. But with a laser you can drill a hole in a diamond or wipe out a cancer.
>
> When you focus a company, you create the same effect. You create a powerful, laserlike ability to dominate a market. That's what focusing is all about.

Focusing itself, however, is dependent on the exercise of a set of secondary skills such as sifting, prioritizing, clustering, chunking, aligning, and sequencing. These are the skills that are called upon in tackling the tasks in this element. Focusing involves the application of these skills in order to be able to give your fullest possible attention to a manageable set of priority goals. Fusion is the name of the game: the object is to generate highly concentrated change initiatives that, like lasers, use up little power but have high intensity and impact. Senge (1990) talks about his "twin-tab" theory in similar terms and Bellamy (in Bellamy, Sinisi, and Holly, 1997) argues for getting the "biggest bang for the buck." None of this is possible, however, without using data to understand needs and create a sense of priority. Data help to unify both the changes and the change makers.

When it comes to the artistry of school improvement, "less is more" is an essential principle of procedure. No matter how counter-intuitive it may sound (when there is so much change to be made how can we possibly cut back), it is one of the best-kept secrets of successful change making. If you concentrate on less and do the less really

CHAPTER 2

well, then you'll achieve more. Focusing is the key activity here; focusing, that is, on what really matters—as indicated in the available data. According to Holly (1990):

> It is better to focus on less change but base it on more information...Changes should be needs-based data-driven.

When he introduced these concepts during a teacher workshop, a member of one participating group turned to him and said:

> Let's clarify what you're saying. The purpose of school improvement is to explore avenues to reduce the load in order to be able to do the right things well...to be more accountable for less.

"Absolutely!" he replied. Getting focused entails looking anew at the change agenda, prioritizing the change load, discarding some things—sometimes referred to as "organized abandonment"—and concentrating on the really important things. How do we know they are the important ones? We have to let the data tell us so. Focusing is good for your health (says Gendlin, 1978); because it involves stress reduction, it is also good for your change psychology. You feel better about yourself as a change maker. Joyce, Wolf, and Calhoun (1993) argue that doing fewer things well benefits both the organization and the students. This is true, but there is still a problem to overcome. When Holly explains the importance of the concept of "less is more" to a group of educators, they agree with him one hundred per cent. When he asks, however, "So what will you discard (or, at least, put on the back-burner)?" they find it very difficult to drop their emotional attachment to various initiatives. They agree intellectually, but not emotionally. In fact, if we're not careful, we quickly recreate the original bubble map because different group members have an attachment to each of the different items on the list—which is why they were on there in the first place.

Getting Focused
Task 1—Part 1: Applying Focusing Skills

<u>Purpose:</u> To give participants a major opportunity to take their "full plate" of changes and apply the focusing skills of sifting and prioritizing.

ELEMENT 1

Getting Focused

Grouping: Work individually.

Directions: On your own, look again at the contents of your version of the bubble map and arrange the changes into four lists: the **Essentials** (those changes that constitute the "less" to work on in order to achieve more); those changes that can be placed on the **Back-Burner** and returned to at a later date; the **Discards**; and any **Change Processes** (that may have found their way onto the longer list) that will help us deal with the change content (e.g., school improvement planning). In making your selection, please keep in mind that *both* the largely external demands produced by the current political realities that impinge on your district and the internal, organic needs of your school/district have to be met. Inevitably, some of these decisions will be tough to make.

The purpose of this major task is twofold: to have the opportunity to wrestle with some substantive change issues while learning how to apply the skills that contribute to focusing, particularly sifting and prioritizing. Use the following **Prioritizing Changes— On Your Own** chart to guide your work.

PRIORITIZING CHANGES—ON YOUR OWN			
Essentials	**Back-Burner**	**Discards**	**Change Processes**

25

CHAPTER 2

Getting Focused ■ Task 1—Part 2: Applying Focusing Skills—Sifting and Prioritizing

Grouping: Work with your Learning Team.

Group process strategy: Use a Consensus Building strategy (refer to the **Group Process Guide**).

Directions: After you complete part 1 of Task 1 on your own, come to consensus as a group. This is an ideal task to learn how to create "sufficient consensus." You are advised not to move on until all members of the team can at least "live with" the group decisions—a process that might entail some trimming of the group agenda. Use the following **Prioritizing Changes—Sufficient Consensus** chart to guide your work. Then, as a group, explain why your team made the choices you did and which were the toughest decisions.

Essentials	Back-Burner	Discards	Change Processes

PRIORITIZING CHANGES—SUFFICIENT CONSENSUS

ELEMENT 1

Getting Focused

If you still need convincing...

Several authors have argued the merits for a more focused approach. Fullan (1996) has said that schools need to be "selectively innovative." Schmoker (1996 and 2001), Patterson et al. (1986), and Calhoun (1994 and 1999) have all argued for choosing powerful goals that focus our change efforts. According to Patterson et al.:

> In schools, clear and shared goals provide unity, help channel and target resources within the school program, [and] can foster collaboration and establish criteria for school success that permit assessment of progress.

Schmoker (1996) returns to the theme that goals (and focusing) are good for our health. "Goals drive us," he says. In this context, he refers to the work of psychologist Csikszentmihalyi (1990) who, according to Schmoker:

> ...has made one of the most interesting discoveries in recent times about the connection between goals and happiness: Goals are the stuff of motivation, persistence, and well-being...he discovered that generally what people enjoy most is pursuing a clear, do-able goal that they value. This connection accounts for why many people are as happy or happier at work than at leisure. In the absence of goals, entropy and aimlessness rush in.
>
> Unfortunately, most schools do not make the connection between goals, motivation, and improvement. We have what is perhaps the most striking, contradictory, self-defeating characteristic of schooling and our efforts to improve it: the gap between the need—and intent—to improve academic performance in our schools on the one hand, and the conspicuous and virtual absence of clear, concrete academic goals in most school or district planning efforts on the other. Without explicit learning goals, we are simply not set up and organized for improvement, for results. Only such goals will allow us to analyze, monitor, and adjust practice toward improvement.

CHAPTER 2

Perhaps the most persistent advocate of the focused goal approach is Emily Calhoun. In a published interview with Dennis Sparks (1999), she argued that it is important to narrow our focus to broaden our effectiveness. She talks about the "singular power of one goal" and warns against trying to satisfy everyone by having too many school improvement goals. If you give in to colleagues' demands and have several goals, she says, it becomes impossible for the school to achieve any of them. Indeed, Calhoun concludes:

> One powerful student learning goal is sufficient if the staff is working diligently on it and looking carefully at student performance.

Two other points emerge from her advice to educators. First, the goal should not be too broad for a faculty to engage in serious, in-depth study; more specificity is required than, for example, aiming to improve literacy. The school, she says, needs to get more specific by focusing on goals like improving student writing of informative prose or improving reading comprehension.

Second, by focusing on one specific goal, the participants can put everything in place that will guarantee goal accomplishment. This is the same message as "less is more." It is what Holly (1990) has called being "packaged for success." An integrated package of related changes is put together—in the interests of the goal in question. In order to achieve the desired student performances (inherent in the goal statement), planning, staff development and other resources (including time for staff collaboration), and team work all have to be assembled and aligned in support of the goal. In a school with such an intense, integrated approach, parent involvement, for example, is not an end in itself; it becomes part of the support package and one of the means to achieving the goal. As Calhoun concludes:

> Having the goal helps us focus; then we can push through it to the things that everyone must be doing to bring it into reality.

Guskey (1990), Hatch (2002) and Joyce, Wolf, and Calhoun (1993) have cogently argued the case for creating integrated change packages in the service of goal attainment. Too often, says Hatch, programs are simply added to the many initiatives already in place instead of being integrated into a focused effort. Joyce et al. point out:

> Considering many dimensions of school renewal simultaneously may seem intimidating at first, but it is healthier to face the complexity than to risk failure because we have neglected important components.

ELEMENT 1
Getting Focused

> For example, asking teachers to engage in collective decision making without providing time for meetings can sabotage an otherwise well-designed effort.

There is a precarious, fine line to walk here. "Less is more" really does mean concentrating on *less* school improvement, but marshalling *more* supports to ensure success. The danger is that so many supports have to be put into place that the change overload that the staff members are trying to avoid is in danger of becoming a reality once again. There are no easy answers here. The best solution—working on enough integrated changes that ensure success but don't swamp people in the process—will emerge from the experience of reflective practice. One thing is certain, as Joyce et al. remind us:

> Of all the decisions people make in a self-renewing organization, probably none is more important than selecting initiatives that will pay off in terms of student learning. Teachers as individuals, schools as faculties, and district personnel as coordinators need to be parsimonious about the number of initiatives that are on the table at any one time. Personnel in all three spheres need to use the limited time available that will have a positive impact. To increase the capacity for innovation and then select weak initiatives would be tragic.

Careful prioritization of change initiatives is clearly important. So too is the understanding that goals are targets (the ends) and implementation strategies (the means) are the vehicles for goal accomplishment. Schmoker refers to them as "objectives" and "innovations." One goal may well be supported by several implementation strategies that can be introduced—in a staggered fashion—over time. Indeed, one of the unfortunate by-products of overloaded change efforts is that you never know which component had the greatest impact. At least this staggered, layered approach to implementation provides you with the luxury of being able to track this question of impact unimpeded by the simultaneous implementation of multiple initiatives.

CHAPTER 2

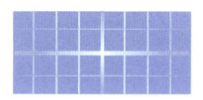

Getting Focused ▪ Task 2: Recognizing the Developmental Stages of Change

<u>Purpose:</u> To use the focusing skills of sifting and sequencing to recognize that various changes are at different stages of development—and that some changes fall into the "accomplishments" bracket and should be celebrated as such.

<u>Grouping:</u> Work with your Learning Team.

<u>Group process strategy:</u> Use a brainstorming technique (refer to the **Group Process Guide**).

<u>Directions:</u> Working as a team and using the chart found on the next page, the task is to become more focused in your change efforts by using a basic sifting and sequencing process. Follow these steps:

1. Select whether you are going to work at the district or school building level.

2. Before starting this task, review the contents of your "bubble map" from Chapter One and what you did with it earlier in this element.

3. Brainstorm a list of items for each column of the sifting chart. (Remember that, when brainstorming, all suggestions are accepted for inclusion and editing is not allowed.)

- In the **Accomplishments** column list all those changes that have occurred in your district/school over the last five to seven years and that have been successfully implemented. These changes—while completed—may still be in need of maintenance, but don't need to be retained in the main body of your school improvement plan.

- In the **Unfinished Business** column list all those changes that have been initiated over the last couple of years and that are still being implemented (therefore, demanding our fullest attention). These changes are in midstream and too important to let go.

- In the **New Emerging Data/Issues** column list any new issues that are on your radar screen, but need to be studied and explored first—prior to implementation.

- In the **Suggested New Goals** column list a few items that, provisionally anyway, look as though they will need to become your next school improvement goals.

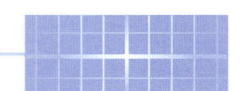

ELEMENT 1
Getting Focused

LEVELS OF PROGRESS	Accomplishments	Unfinished Business	New Emerging Data/Issues	Suggested New Goals
District				
Building				

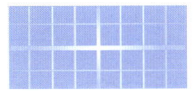

Getting Focused
Task 3: Planning and Sequencing Changes Over Time

<u>Purpose:</u> To undertake another activity that calls on the focusing skills of planning and being intentional by sequencing the changes over time.

<u>Grouping:</u> Work individually or in Learning Teams.

CHAPTER 2

Directions: This task is centered on the skills of sequencing and staggering the changes over time. In Dubuque Schools, Dubuque, Iowa, major initiatives are staggered across various years using the SEIM matrix planner. In the acronym SEIM, 'S' stands for **Study**, 'E' for **Early Implementation**, 'I' for fuller **Implementation**, and 'M' for **Maintenance**. Activities are arranged in such a way that no two initiatives are receiving the same kind of treatment at the same time. How might this work for you? On the chart below, enter a schedule for the initiatives that you identified in Task 2 that is appropriate for your situation.

SCHOOL INITIATIVES OVER TIME

	Current School Year _____	_____	_____	_____	_____
Study					
Early Implementation					
Implementation					
Maintenance					

ELEMENT 1
Getting Focused

Getting Focused
Task 4: Clustering Changes

Purpose: To learn how to cluster changes by identifying which changes are supports and which are major initiatives.

Grouping: Work individually or in Learning Teams.

Directions: The task this time is to use the skills of chunking, synthesizing, and aligning by taking one of the key initiatives from the previous task and building on the advice of Calhoun (1999) and Holly (1990).

1. Identify and record below the **Major Goal**, concentrating on this one area (e.g., improving reading comprehension).

2. Identify some support activities that would enhance the concentrated approach by providing four kinds of support using the 4Cs Frame: **Curriculum and Instruction**, **Climate for Learning**, **Student Competencies**, and **Collaboration**.

Major Goal:

SUPPORT ACTIVITIES			
Curriculum and Instruction	**Climate**	**Competencies**	**Collaboration**

33

CHAPTER 2

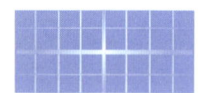

Getting Focused
Task 5: How to Say "No"

<u>Purpose:</u> To practice the art of saying "no" in non-confrontational ways.

<u>Grouping:</u> Work in pairs or triads, followed by a Learning Team sharing time.

<u>Directions:</u> Given that there are so many demands for change and that it is tough to apply the "less is more" approach, we all need to practice how to say "no" in non-confrontational ways. For example, "Let's study it first" is an often-used delaying tactic that, for several reasons, is actually rather smart. After all, it is often good to study things first and not leap headlong (and unprepared) into wholesale change. So this is your chance to come up with other comments, expressions, and statements that help you to disagree — with the pace and amount of change — in agreeable ways. Disagreeing agreeably is a key skill in school improvement. Work with one or two people in creating your own statements. Then, meet together with the other members of your Learning Team to share your statements.

Delaying Effect	Comments, Expressions, Statements	Change Effect
For example: Avoid having to do anything immediately.	"Let's study it first."	Allows a more reflective and planned implementation.

CHANGE LOG
Getting Focused

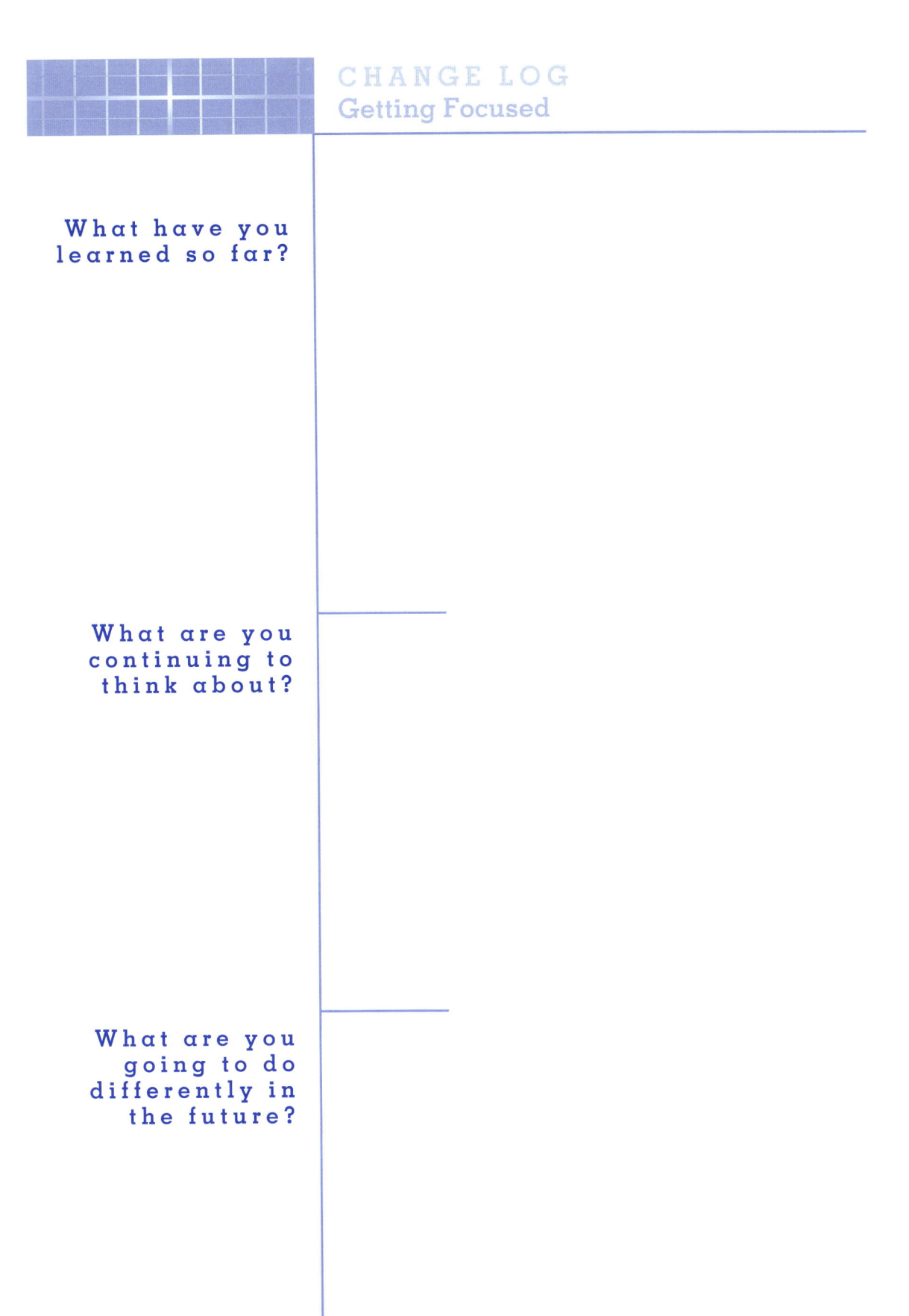

What have you learned so far?

What are you continuing to think about?

What are you going to do differently in the future?

CHANGE LOG
Getting Focused

Notes

ELEMENT 2
Creating a Shared Agenda

Overview

Focusing is both a question of substance (what) and allegiance (who). A focused agenda, by definition, has to be a shared one. For instance, when Goodlad (1984) talks about a school's "hard-rock agenda" for change, he has both meanings in mind: the agenda should be highly focused and have the solidarity of support that comes with it being commonly agreed upon. Such an agreement should be wrought through the agency of a participatory process. This is why participatory decision making and group processing have such a crucial role to play—in providing a collaborative, inclusive process from which the shared agreements can emerge. It has been said that the best (that is, shared) decision is one that no one has in mind when entering the room. In other words, the final decision should emerge from the dialogue and be a genuine product of the group and its processing—with everyone present feeling that they have contributed to the decision, but no one person present feeling that his or her pre-existing agenda "won the day."

The same applies to a change agenda; the best agenda emerges from the group members' deliberation—and their scrutiny of the available data—and is not imposed on the group by any one of its members or, indeed, any sub-group of members. Moreover, the focus grows not only from the group's deliberation but also from the coalescence of the members' experience, enthusiasm, and enlightenment. Participation in the process of data use brings people on board; their sifting of informed choices gives them ownership, engagement, and a collective resolve to get something done. Focused and shared decision making is a highly skilled activity. The skills that are required include: data processing; connecting, clustering, and integrating issues; shared, participatory decision making; collaborative reflection; and reaching "sufficient consensus" by jelling disparate viewpoints into a sufficiently common-ground agenda.

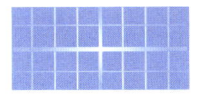

Creating a Shared Agenda
Task 1: Instant Gardening

<u>Purpose:</u> To learn the importance and inter-connectedness of ownership, involvement, and responsibility.

<u>Grouping:</u> First work individually, then in pairs, and then pairs sharing with pairs.

<u>Directions:</u> To introduce this element, you are asked to silently read the passage that follows and then respond to some questions that are meant to trigger your personal reflection.

CHAPTER 2

In the U.K. one of the most popular television programs for several years has been a gardening program called "Ground Force." The idea for the program is very simple. Selected homeowners (to whom the service is offered free of charge) are asked to leave for a couple of days and a team moves in to do a total makeover of the yard—including flower beds, grassed areas, trees and bushes, paths, ornamental rockeries and ponds. Part of the program's attraction is that the team is working to the clock, has to deal with all the vicissitudes that the weather and the seasons can bring, and has to have departed by the time the homeowners return to inspect their new, surprise "instant garden."

As a result of the program, a new industry has been spawned—called naturally enough "instant gardening." Companies have been formed that specialize in total yard make-overs—without, however, incorporating some of the element of surprise built into the television program and, not surprisingly, charging very high fees for their services. In the gardening magazines, this new industry has taken much criticism from the so-called traditionalists who, for various reasons, find the "instant gardening" approach somewhat distasteful. Moreover, early research on the instant gardens themselves (especially, but not exclusively, those produced for television) is not encouraging. It would suggest that, within a very short space of time, the new gardens are left to rapidly deteriorate—much to the delight of the traditionalists who are able to announce, "We told you so."

First respond on your own to the following questions, then discuss the questions with a partner in your team, followed by a sharing/discussion with another dyad in order to gradually develop a common set of ideas and issues.

1. Why do you think the traditional gardeners have been so critical of this new approach?

ELEMENT 2
Creating a Shared Agenda

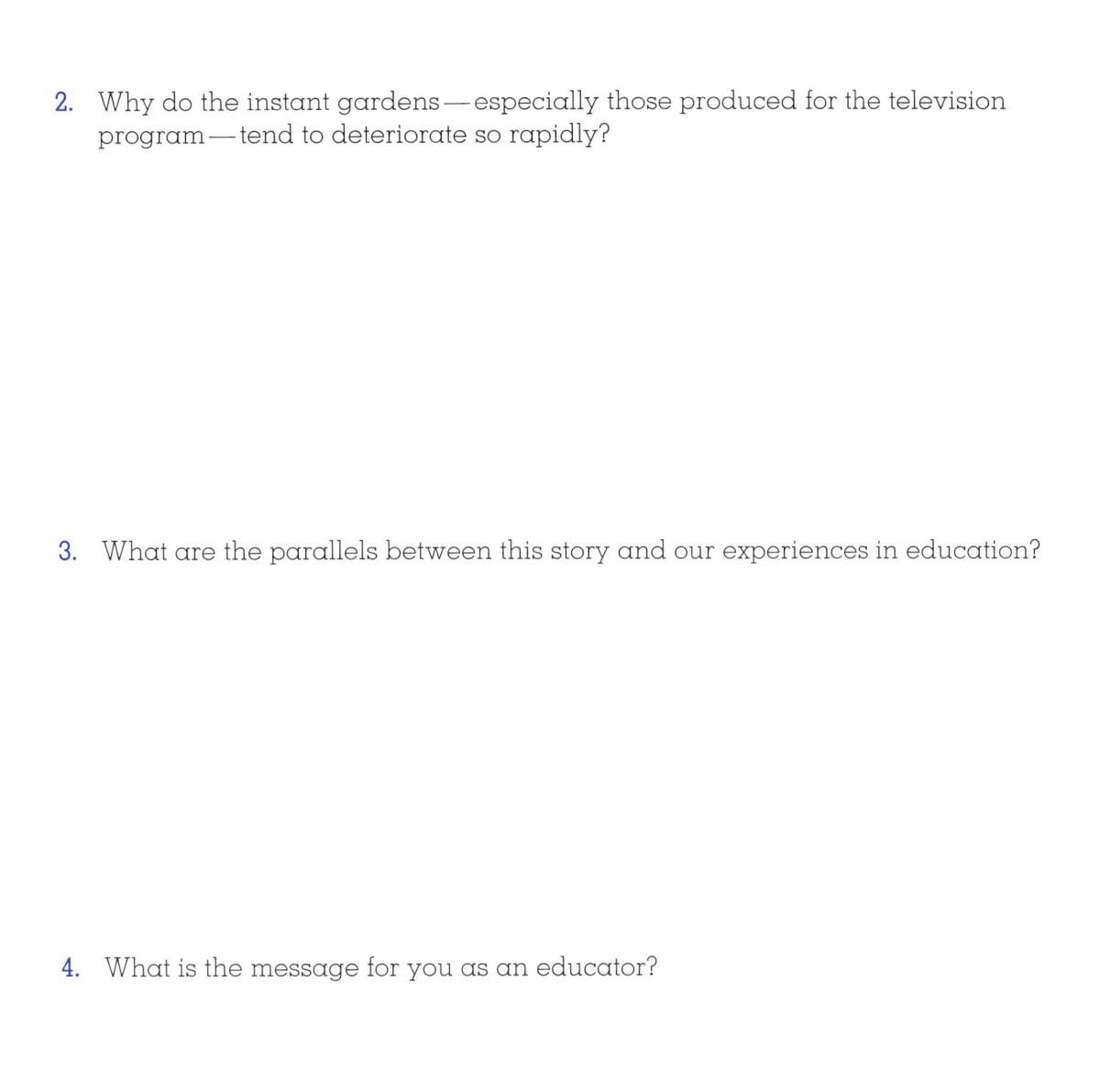

2. Why do the instant gardens—especially those produced for the television program—tend to deteriorate so rapidly?

3. What are the parallels between this story and our experiences in education?

4. What is the message for you as an educator?

Six Factors That Contribute to a Healthy Life

Sometimes the best way to learn about ourselves as educators is to study other spheres of human activity and draw the parallels in our behavior—as you just did above. This approach allows us to distance ourselves from our immediate context and look back in at ourselves with a clearer pair of eyes. What is somewhat discouraging—but perhaps strangely heartwarming—is that, when it comes to change, we all make the same mistakes. In industry and management (despite claims to the contrary), in hospitals and churches, in private and public services, when it comes to change, we often forget to apply the basic principles of human psychology. We learned in dealing with Element One that, while we may think that we have to meet all the change demands that come along, the actual case is that we cannot afford to try and meet them all at any one time—and still be successful.

So what do we know about basic human needs that can be of service to us? We know—and these understandings have been recently confirmed in brain research and resiliency theory—that human beings need to feel that

- they are *informed* and "in the know;"
- they are able to make *choices;*
- they have a sense of being in *control;*
- they have *ownership* of what's going on;
- they are participating as effective members of a *team* in something worthwhile;
- they are making a contribution to the creation of a *shared agenda.*

The following figure depicts the relationship of these six variables.

Six Factors for a Healthy Life

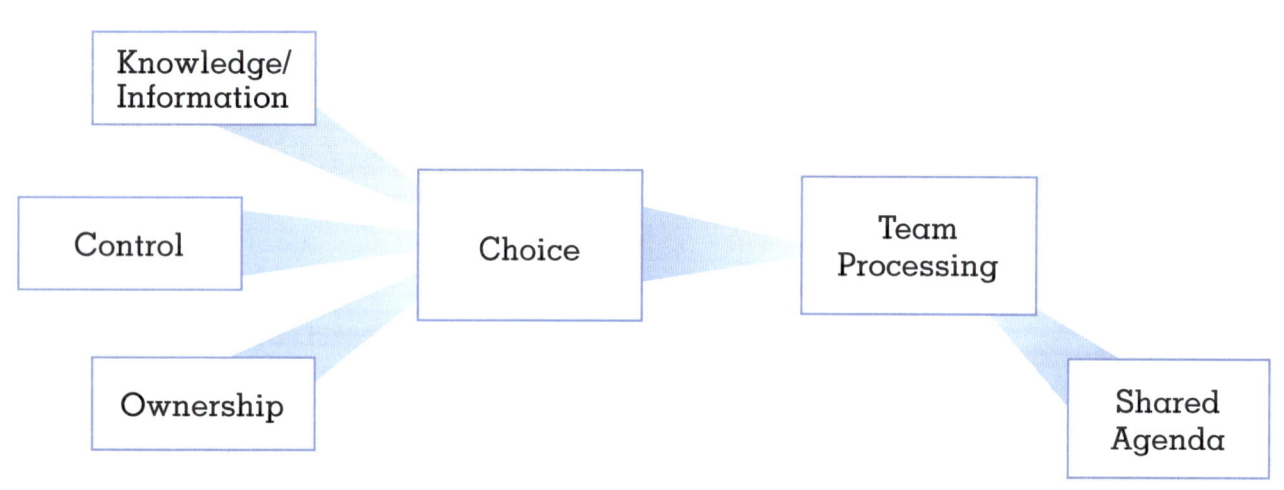

```
  Knowledge/
  Information

  Control          Choice          Team
                                   Processing

  Ownership                        Shared
                                   Agenda
```

ELEMENT 2

Creating a Shared Agenda

We can only make good choices on the basis of sound information. If we're kept in the dark and denied access to knowledge and information, we do not know what options are available to us. Argyris and Schon (1978) talk about the importance of being able to make "free and informed choices." Such choices, they say, are based on valid information, the use of which enables us to be mindful, conscious, and intentional in our decision making. Choice involves careful selection; careful selection involves thought; thought involves processing ideas; and ideas come from data. The prudent, informed choice, therefore, is guided by data. Moreover, the exercise of choice has various repercussions. For a start we feel more proactive, more in the driver's seat, and, therefore, more in control. The whole approach introduced in this workbook is predicated on the notion presented by Holly (1990):

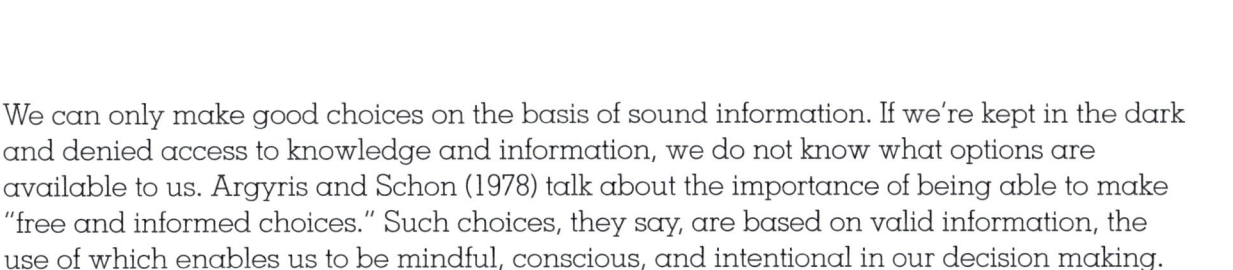

> **It is better to be a controller of change than a victim of change.**

Conner (1995) clearly agrees. He says that human beings are control-oriented and need to feel in charge of events. Conner also points out that if people are unable to deal with the amount of change, they begin to display dysfunctional behaviors. The task, he says, is to help people absorb change while minimizing the dysfunctionalism. Part of the answer to this conundrum is the creation of *internal control* (which includes the acceptance of personal responsibility and accountability) in each individual teacher and each school. Then, as Roland Barth (1991) has argued, change can come from within—however much it is stimulated from the outside. It is the response to change (the control mechanism) that has to come from within. We have to engage change, says Conner, rather than automatically defend against it. Indeed, it is the act of engagement that provides us with a sense of ownership. The quickest way to ownership is by working hard on—and personally investing in—a successful project. It is your creation, of which you are justly proud, and because of which you have a real sense of achievement. Yet this does not have to be an individual pursuit; working successfully on a team project can evoke the same feelings.

Indeed, according to Schmoker (1996) and Csikszentmihalyi (1990), working within the *flow* of an effective team process can heighten the elation that comes with a sense of accomplishment. This is where effective group processing becomes so important—so participants feel that they are both engaged and making valid contributions. Individuals do not have to totally control the agenda; they need to feel that they made an important contribution to what is a shared agenda.

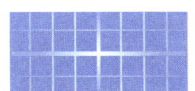

Creating a Shared Agenda ■ Task 2: Relating the Six Factors for a Healthy Life to Professional Situations

<u>Purpose:</u> To apply six factors that contribute to a healthy organizational life to participants' own professional situations—and to learn the skills of active listening at the same time.

CHAPTER 2

Note: Tasks 2 and 3 work in tandem and constitute a major undertaking for your team.

Grouping: Work individually and then in pairs.

Directions: Working individually, think about your **current professional situation** in terms of the six factors mentioned above (being in the know, having choices, feeling in control, having a sense of ownership, team membership, and making a contribution to a shared agenda) and respond in writing to the following four questions. Then, working in pairs, share your written responses with each other. You will need to listen carefully and perhaps make notes. You will be asked to speak for *your partner* (and he or she for you) in the next stage of the activity.

1. What is happening in your current situation?

2. Is it a positive or negative experience (or both)? Why?

3. How are the six factors contributing to the nature of the experience?

4. How do you feel about your involvement in the situation?

ELEMENT 2

Creating a Shared Agenda

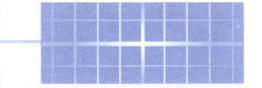

Creating a Shared Agenda ▪ Task 3: Creating a Central List of Common Ground Issues

Purpose: To apply a consensus-building strategy to the issues that emerged from the previous exercise and generate a shared agenda.

Grouping: Work with your Learning Team. A recorder will need to be selected.

Group process strategy: Use the Tambourine strategy (refer to the **Group Process Guide**).

Directions: Use the Tambourine strategy to share your reflections from the previous task and create a central list of common ground issues. For this activity, *your partner speaks for you* during the initial stage of the Tambourine. Concentrate on how the six factors impact your current professional lives—which ones are working for you and which ones are not. In terms of the common ground issues, aim to end up with two lists under the sub-headings **Strengths** and **Challenges**. Select a team member to act as the recorder. As a follow-up activity, your team could discuss how the Tambourine strategy could be applied in other circumstances.

Matching the Best of the Old with the Best of the New

The creation of a shared change agenda should involve two other major considerations:

- What has previously been referred to as the Culture of Innovation (Holly and Southworth, 1989) involves a near obsession with the pursuit of the new. The attitude seems to be that if any ideas, strategies, and programs that we use are older than one year then they must be obsolete. The Culture of Development, on the other hand, deliberately embraces the best of both worlds, the tried-and-true and the contemporary. As has been argued elsewhere (Holly, 1990):

> Effective change is a combination of the best of the old and the best of the new.

- John Goodlad (1984) argued that a school's improvement plan should encapsulate its "hard rock agenda" for change—one that combines both internal and external agendas. Every school is the object of external pressures (including state and federal mandates) and the subject of internal needs and deficiencies. The secret is in the blending of the two agendas.

CHAPTER 2

When talking to educators at the start of a major change initiative, they often admit to three common fears: this initiative is yet another reform being foisted on them—to add to the existing pile; roles and responsibilities are unclear ("What," they ask, "is expected of us?"); and, above all, everything they've done before is being ignored and, therefore, devalued. The Culture of Innovation, teachers say, seems to delight in "throwing the baby out with the bath water" (a frequent comment). Unfortunately, this is a sad but true state of affairs, as the author's following narrative testifies.

> One Monday morning I was scheduled to lead a school improvement workshop in Scotland, but, because of inclement weather, my flight from London was delayed. In the rush to get to the conference location—where some four hundred people were waiting—the usual briefing by the workshop organizers was curtailed. One of them, however, insisted on giving a warning; that, in the audience, there was a school principal (an "old curmudgeon" was the way he was described) who had not been to a workshop for thirty-two years and, because he had been forced to attend this event, had threatened to tear the workshop leader apart limb by limb—metaphorically-speaking, of course. Given the haste to get started, the warning slipped from my mind.
>
> I started by introducing myself and some of my beliefs about educational change—including the importance of combining "the best of the old with the best of the new." For some subconscious reason, I included the comment, that, when it comes to school improvement, everyone counts: we need, I said, to get everyone in the game—the old and the young—so as to benefit from the widest possible range of experience, expertise, and enthusiasm. "We have to grow from well-established roots."
>
> No sooner had these words left my mouth than I was interrupted by a loud shout from the back of the room. The principal—about whom I had been warned—rose to his feet and addressed the audience. He opened his speech by inviting the entire audience to "Listen to this speaker; he's talking good common

ELEMENT 2

Creating a Shared Agenda

sense!" He slightly altered the truth by adding, "This is the best workshop I've ever been to." I wanted to reply, "Actually, it's the only workshop!" but I held my tongue. The principal then sat down and the workshop continued.

At the next break I engaged my newfound ally in conversation. "Why," I asked "did you feel moved to speak the way you did?" "It's quite simple," the seasoned campaigner replied, "You are the first person who has come in here and a) did not offer yet another sole remedy for our problems and b) said that much of what has happened previously should be honored and retained." He also threw in for good measure that, "All these changes that we're now being asked to do have been here several times before — the names have changed but the activities are the same. If they were important enough to introduce the first time, why were they let go — only to be recycled several times over?"

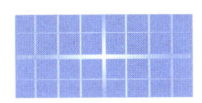

Creating a Shared Agenda
Task 4: Listening to Others' Views and Opinions

Purpose: To learn the importance of listening to views and opinions that are divergent from our own.

Grouping: Work with your Learning Team. Select a recorder.

Group processing strategy: Use a brainstorming technique.

CHAPTER 2

Directions: The author has retold the previous story many times and teachers always seem to respond positively. What in the principal's reaction strikes a chord with educators everywhere? As a team, brainstorm some ideas and have a recorder list them on chart paper. Also, as a team, respond to the following questions:

1. For the purposes of learning, why is it better to be surrounded by people who potentially disagree with you?

2. What does this tell us about forming teams?

Brainstorming notes:

ELEMENT 2

Creating a Shared Agenda

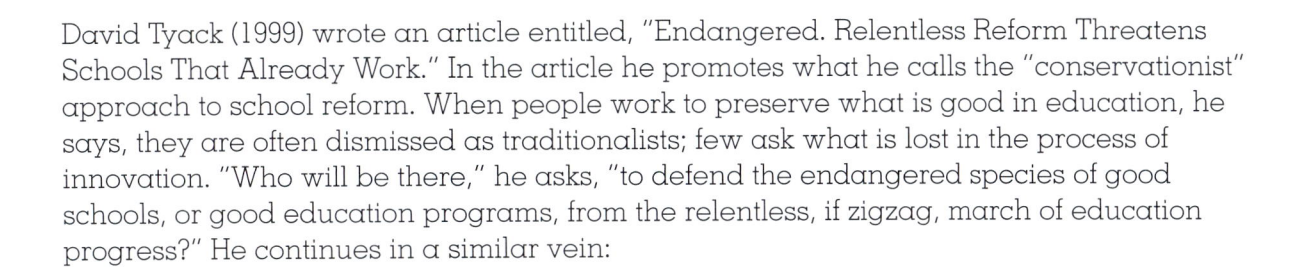

David Tyack (1999) wrote an article entitled, "Endangered. Relentless Reform Threatens Schools That Already Work." In the article he promotes what he calls the "conservationist" approach to school reform. When people work to preserve what is good in education, he says, they are often dismissed as traditionalists; few ask what is lost in the process of innovation. "Who will be there," he asks, "to defend the endangered species of good schools, or good education programs, from the relentless, if zigzag, march of education progress?" He continues in a similar vein:

> Those who believe in progress through education reform often want to reinvent schooling. According to them, the dead hand of the past has created problems for rational planners to solve in the future. These innovators follow a predictable pattern: First, they exaggerate defects in order to raise alarm; then, they try to wipe the slate clean; finally, they propose a short time frame for their favorite solution, hoping to see results before the next election or job opportunity or grant proposal.
>
> The ideology of progress through change obscures what a 'conservationist' strategy illuminates: **It is at least as important to conserve the good as to invent the new.** It is easy to become so obsessed with what is not working—the cacophony of bad schools—that one forgets what makes many schools sing. Good schools are hard to create and nurture, for they require healthy relationships of trust, challenge, and respect—qualities that take time to grow. When teachers, students, parents, and administrators create such learning communities, a conservationist strategy seeks to preserve what makes them work, to sabotage ignorant efforts to 'fix what ain't broke,' and to share knowledge about how to grow more such places.
>
> It seeks to moderate the pendulum swings of policies that decree that schools should be larger (or smaller), that more (or fewer) courses should be elective, or that governance should be more (or less) centralized.

Tyack adds two other comments that are crucial to the purpose of this workbook. First, he says, the conservationist analyzes as well as advocates. By this comment he means that the analysis of data shows what is working and what should, therefore, be retained and, indeed, championed. Some schools, according to his thesis, are already treasuries of good practice—as the evidence proves. Second, the conservationist cannot look only

CHAPTER 2

backward, for preservation also involves planning for the future. By this comment, Tyack would seem to be endorsing the "best of the old and best of the new" approach by arguing that our school improvement plans should contain what is known to work already—alongside and integrated with the known best of the new—in the service of the future and other generations of students.

Returning to Goodlad's point—school improvement plans should contain a focused and shared "hard rock agenda" that is a blend of the external and the internal—it seems reasonable to suggest that the best of the old is likely to emerge from an analysis of internal data and the best of the new will emerge from the scanning of external data. Thus a school can build on existing strengths—as identified in the internal data—and become even stronger by incorporating and blending new ideas and strategies found in a trawl of the external data. The Developing School, with a Development Culture, is always looking to blend continuity and change, the old and the new, the proven and the recommended, what has worked here and what has evidently worked elsewhere.

You will find below a chart that attempts to summarize the differences between the Innovation Culture and the Development Culture. The two lists have been deliberately polarized in order to bring out the differences.

The Innovation Culture	The Development Culture
Short-term, quick fix, project mentality	Long-term, long haul approach
Faddist, superficial, fragmentary; 'flavor of the month'	Best of old and best of new; integrated package
Too much too fast; here today and gone tomorrow	Sustained, focused, deeper commitment
Arbitrary whims; latest bright ideas — unfiltered and random	Needs-based data-driven; purposeful; vision is the filter
Lack of planning, preparation, training, lead-in time	Packaged for success; "less is more" approach
Resources frittered away — too few resources chasing too many innovations	Focused resources — pooled at point of need; aligned with needs and goals
No data; no sense of need; no tracking of progress	Changes grounded in data — at every step
Means treated as ends in themselves; solutions looking for problems	Means selected to meet ends
No change theory, no learning theory	Change-as-learning theory

ELEMENT 2

Creating a Shared Agenda

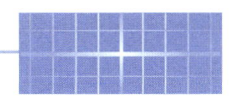

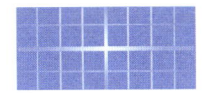

Creating a Shared Agenda ▪ Task 5: Rating Your School's Current Approach to Change

Purpose: To provide participants with an important opportunity to reflect on and rate (on a 1-5 scale) their school's current approach to change.

Grouping: Work with your Learning Team.

Directions: As a Learning Team, think about your current educational situation. What aspects of the Innovation Culture does your school/school district possess and what aspects of the Development Culture are in place? Using the "rating scales" included below, assess the current reality of your school's approach to change.

Short-term, quick fix mentality				Long-term, long-haul approach
1	2	3	4	5

Faddist, superficial, fragmentary				Integrating best of old and new
1	2	3	4	5

Too much too fast				Focused, sustained commitment
1	2	3	4	5

Unfiltered, random ideas				Needs-based data-driven
1	2	3	4	5

Lack of planning and preparation				Packaged for success
1	2	3	4	5

Resources frittered away				Aligned use of resources
1	2	3	4	5

No data; no sense of need				Changes grounded in data
1	2	3	4	5

Means treated as ends				Means selected to meet ends
1	2	3	4	5

No change or learning theories				Change-as-learning theory
1	2	3	4	5

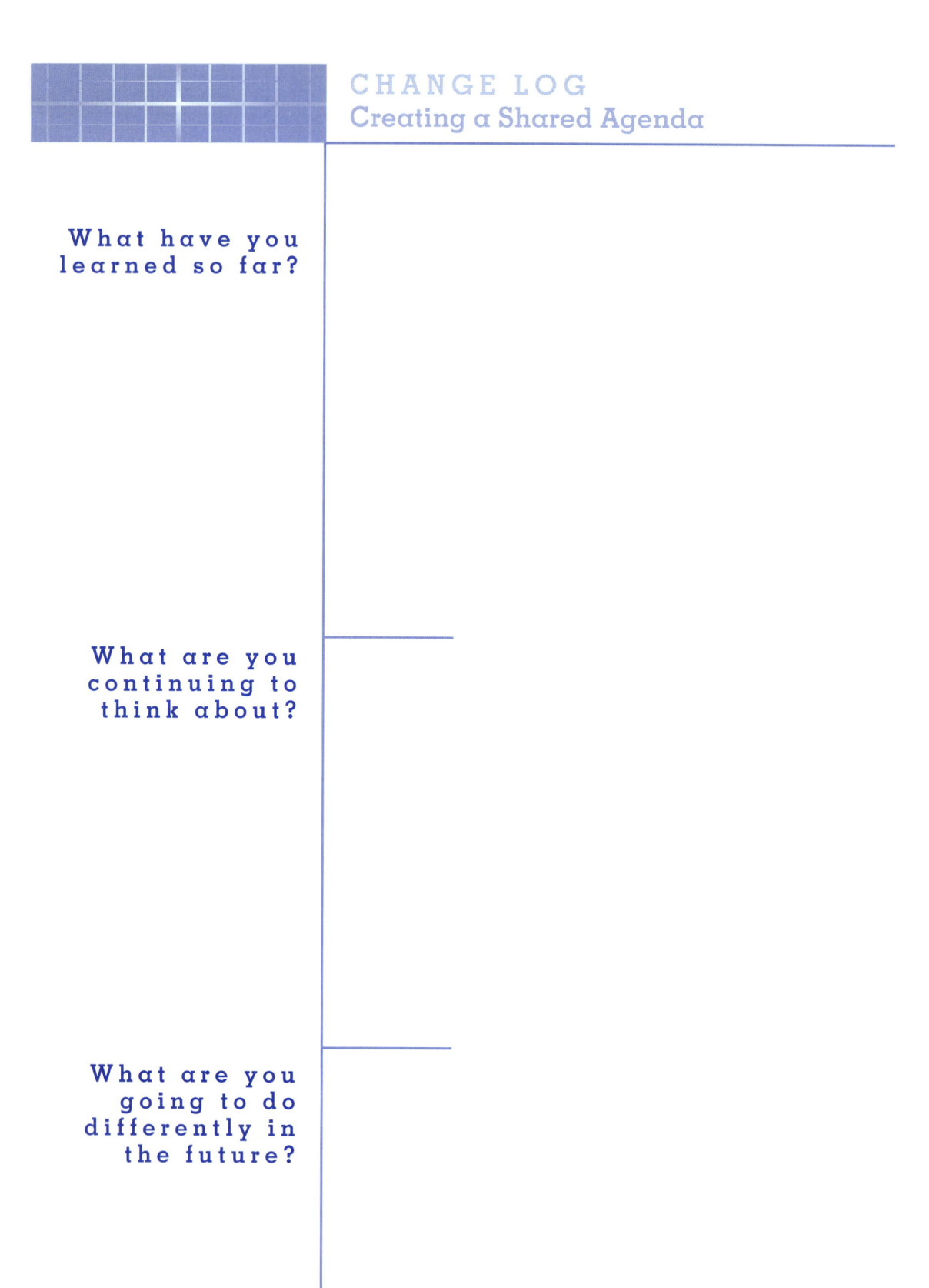

CHANGE LOG
Creating a Shared Agenda

What have you learned so far?

What are you continuing to think about?

What are you going to do differently in the future?

ELEMENT 3

Follow-Through—Sustaining Changes Over Time

Overview

Educators often complain that we give up on changes too easily and that we don't make the most of the current changes before the next ones come along. While there is much evidence to support this claim, what educators sometimes fail to understand is that sustained change efforts are exactly that—sustained efforts. You have to keep working on them, all the while being open to the possibility of having to make so-called in-flight adjustments—in the light of feedback data. Sustainment and flexibility are both essential skills to use during the process of implementation and they are not as contradictory as they might sound. The one speaks to the importance of long-term commitment and the other to the need to make adjustments and accommodations in order to ensure eventual success. Goals are the immutable ends; strategies are the variable—and, therefore, changeable—means. Essential skills in this area include progress monitoring and the applied use of feedback data. What is also required is the mindset of an action researcher. During implementation and follow-through, participants—like good sailors—need to keep asking themselves whether it would be more productive to keep sailing forward or to change tack.

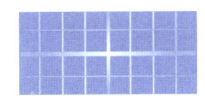

Follow-Through
Task 1: Changing Trains—a Metaphor

Purpose: To learn through the power of analogy that, once we've embarked on them, we have to sustain our changes over time.

Grouping: Work individually and then with your Learning Team.

Directions: As an introduction to this element, read the following passage and answer the three questions that follow it. Reflect individually and then share your reflections with the members of your Learning Team.

Changing Trains

> You are in Chicago and you want to get to Los Angeles. Having studied your travel options, you decide to travel by railroad. You have sufficient time and the price of the ticket better suits your current financial status. In addition, the railroad happens to be your preferred mode of travel. Several days in advance of your journey you buy an Amtrak ticket and

CHAPTER 2

you turn up at the station on the right day and in good time. The train—which you notice is well-used and rather "down-at-heel" (it could certainly be a lot newer and much cleaner)—pulls out on time and moves westward. Its speed is slow but steady. At the first stop—Burlington, Iowa—another train pulls in alongside yours. This other train is brand-spanking new; what's more it is super-clean and looks sleek and rapid. You hear someone further down the car say that this other train is also going to Los Angeles and it's going to get there quicker. You grab your bags, hurtle across the platform, jump on the other train just as it begins to move—and end up in Washington D.C. (Holly, 1996).

1. In what ways is this story a metaphor for the way we often go about change in education?

2. How could using data have improved this situation?

3. What was the real error in the way you decided to change trains in the story?

ELEMENT 3

Follow-Through — Sustaining Changes Over Time

Sustaining Change Efforts

One of your responses to the last question was probably something like, "Quick fixes never work—you have to give changes more time." Absolutely. As Joyce, Wolf, and Calhoun (1993) have said, having studied your change needs and the available strategic options, it would be tragic not to choose a program that stands to make a real difference in terms of student learning. Similarly, once an option has been carefully selected and implementation initiated, it would be equally tragic not to stay the course. Change is for the long haul. And, as many commentators have argued, real change occurs when there is follow-through and sustained implementation. This takes long-term commitment on the part of those involved—which can be triggered by the participants having a hand in the needs identification, prioritization, change selection and planning processes in the first place. As has been said: Involvement generates commitment.

The message is, if you have a hand in the making of something, you are much more inclined to "stick with it" over time. Involvement in the selection of a change effort makes you an investor; you have a vested interest in its long-term success.

This is one area where change theory and teachers' practical interests genuinely coincide. As the members of one school team said to me: We want a school which is innovative and stable. We don't want changes that are here today and gone tomorrow.

The stability that they are looking for is an agreed upon, continuously applied way of going about change. Having embarked on a chosen course, they said, it is imperative that persistence and sustainment be applied to its implementation. While educators dislike the "flavor of the month" approach to change, they have a real aversion to not hanging tough with changes over time. As the saying goes, "If it's worth doing, it's worth doing properly."

Follow-Through
Task 2: Sustaining Changes Over Time

Purpose: To learn the skill of deep listening while reflecting on what it takes to sustain the change process over time.

LT

Grouping: Work with your Learning Team.

CHAPTER 2

<u>Group process strategy:</u> Sitting in your Circle configuration, you have an excellent opportunity to practice a new skill. Each time a team member makes a contribution, the next person to speak has to respond *directly* to the previous speaker. This dignifies the contribution of each speaker, increases the connectedness and relevance of the discussion, and erases "bird-walks" and the exercise of personal agendas.

<u>Directions:</u> In your Learning Team, discuss the two questions included below.

1. What does it take to stick to a change over time?

2. What might prevent us from following through with a particular change? Why?

It's a case of staying the course, but...

There is, however, another aspect to keep in mind. In order to achieve long-term success it might prove prudent—in the light of feedback—to alter course slightly. If the first Los Angeles train develops engine trouble, then changing trains—to one that is definitely going to Los Angeles (or even one that is going to Los Angeles via Albuquerque)—might be a viable option. While it is prudent to stick with a robust, impactful change all the way, it is equally prudent not to slavishly adhere to a change that is going nowhere fast. A sensible middle course is to stick with the original change, but, in the light of feedback data, adjust the way in which it is working so it is more on target. It is a classic characteristic of accomplished teachers who adjust their lessons based on feedback during implementation. Teachers also adjust instruction based on assessment data. Indeed, this willingness to make adjustments and adaptations while in motion is a classic characteristic of successful change making. Put simply, it is the learning journey to your chosen destination that is all-important; actually getting there might involve several strategic twists and turns. It all hinges on the need to succeed. In the pursuit of success, it often pays to be strategically flexible in the light of local knowledge and cultural norms.

Milbrey McLaughlin (1987) has reminded us that implementation dominates outcomes. Federal and state policymakers, she says, cannot mandate what matters at the local level. When teachers fail to carry out policy directives fully or faithfully, they may be responding in the only way they can. Moreover, she says, they may well have assessed that the new practices are not as good as the ones being replaced. Problems, she says, are never solved; rather they evolve through a "multi-staged, iterative process" with new issues emerging as the process unfolds. She states:

> This kind of creeping, locally defined change is often for the best.

ELEMENT 3
Follow-Through — Sustaining Changes Over Time

According to McLaughlin, there are countless combinations and permutations of practice to be tried and tested and it is the ongoing process of feedback looping that makes it a learning journey for those involved. As McLaughlin concludes:

> Learning from experience, then, requires...a model of social learning and policy analysis that stresses reflection and assistance to ongoing decision making...Strategies for analysis and evaluation might become self-consciously multi-staged, developmental and iterative, keying questions and methodologies to the point in the process under study, to the needs of key decision makers, and establishing a regularized system of feedback to actors at all levels of the system.

Henry Mintzberg in his seminal article entitled, "The Fall and Rise of Strategic Planning" (1994) covers much the same ground as McLaughlin. He makes three points that have great relevance:

1. Strategic planning in education usually involves a formalized, rational sequence from analysis through administrative procedure to eventual action. But strategy making as a learning process, he says, can proceed in the other direction too. In his words:

   > We think in order to act, to be sure, but we also act in order to think. We try things, and those experiments that work converge gradually into viable patterns that become strategies. This is the very essence of strategy making as a learning process.

   What is exciting about this notion is that it is very close to the way that teachers actually perform in the classroom. They make countless small moves and experiments and retain the ones that work the best. "The big picture," says Mintzberg, "is painted with little strokes." What is important, he emphasizes, is the commitment to a learning journey and the willingness to undertake flexible strategizing. It is the synthesis of what works over time that constitutes the learning. This is the underpinning of the scientific method — another familiar metaphor for teachers.

2. What is required, he says, is common direction (vision, goals) and individual discretion over how to get there; individual pursuit should not be over-controlled. Charles Handy (1984), the author's mentor in England, has always said that we over-control the "how" in education and under-control the "what" (we want to achieve) and it should be the other way round. There should be tightness of direction and looseness of ways to accomplish it. This acknowledgment that there are different routes to the same goal

does not mean a lack of accountability, but rather more accountability. We are all accountable for reaching the commonly agreed goals—by using whatever means we deem desirable—and have to be able to show that our strategies do, indeed, "deliver the goods." It also means, of course, that different teachers in the same school could be using very different teaching methods—but are still part of the same accountability system and working to the same goals. What Handy (1984) has called using simultaneous tight-loose properties creates tightness of purpose yet releases staff member initiative—and choice—rather than stifling it. Mintzberg concludes:

> When an organization conveys the message that it does not depend on people in any significant way, the sensible human response for workers is to disengage from the organization....When the structures and processes of work are standardized, no room exists for difference. Viewing people as the means to organizational ends protects the organization from variations among workers, quiets dissenting voices, and flattens affective responses to organizational purposes and directions. The cost of this insurance is high, however. The organization loses the creativity and ingenuity of its people, and individuals lose their sense of efficacy and their opportunities for connection with others who share a common purpose.

Mintzberg's comments really add to the understanding of one of the central change dilemmas. It is widely believed that when people in schools are treated well, they will respond to change in positive ways. Experience in schools suggests, however, that this is not always the case. Even when treated well—and certainly better than what was previously the case—educators can still react in somewhat surly, unforgiving ways. Indeed, their behavior may actually worsen. What Mintzberg points out is that the "extent to which individuals in subordinate roles avoid responsibility or lack ambition would appear to be a consequence of past opportunity and experience, not an inherent characteristic." Given a history of negative experiences, it takes more time than we realize to undo the distrust and unlearn all the diversionary habits that were acquired. Indeed, especially during the "release" period, it would be unwise to expect old habits to disappear over night.

3. Cooperative school environments, says Mintzberg, bring people together while protecting diversity of experience, preference, and interest. School improvement efforts, he says, should create collegial, supportive work environments and foster the sharing of ideas, while allowing individual difference to be a strength not a weakness. Respect for individual differences, he tells us, should be a cornerstone of educational change. Ten years ago, as part of the Schools for the Twenty-First Century initiative in

ELEMENT 3
Follow-Through—Sustaining Changes Over Time

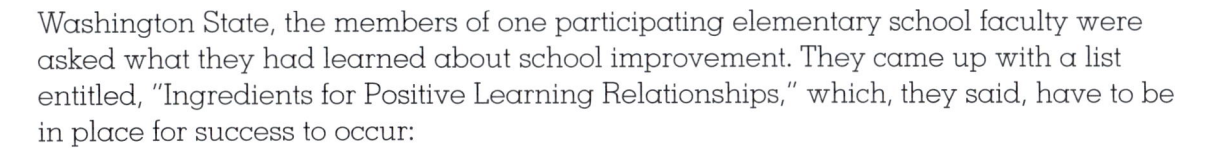

Washington State, the members of one participating elementary school faculty were asked what they had learned about school improvement. They came up with a list entitled, "Ingredients for Positive Learning Relationships," which, they said, have to be in place for success to occur:

- trust
- need/readiness
- positive climate/attitudes
- support/encouragement
- flexibility to personalize
- time to practice/internalize
- respecting others' strengths/weaknesses
- freedom to make, and learn from, mistakes
- celebrations/sharing of successes

Revisiting this list it is interesting to note how much they got it right and how much they approached school improvement, to use Mintzberg's phrase, as a learning journey—collaboratively and individually.

Both McLaughlin and Mintzberg remind us that successful change making often requires reconciling ideas that would seem to be opposites. In the case of "sticking to our changes over time," we now have two seemingly contradictory ideas with which to contend. One is that, having carefully selected a particular change, it has to be the subject of your devotion and commitment for some considerable time. The other is that it is important to be flexible and to be prepared to change the change and make what have been called "in-flight adjustments" in the light of accumulating feedback data. Grit and determination, as opposed to blinkered obstinacy, are certainly necessary to be able to stick with a particular change over the long haul—even if, at first, the data are not exactly positive. As Rosabeth Moss Kanter (1983) has observed:

Everything looks like a failure in the middle.

Continuing to disregard danger signals can, of course, prove disastrous. It is the student learning goals to which we owe our relentless, long-term commitment. Part of our problem is that we often confuse goals and strategies and become too wedded to our strategies. Yes, we have to make every effort to make them work, and then, if they are not (according to the data), we make adjustments to make sure that they do. In a previous book, the author (1999) lists the attributes and attitudes (the mindset) of an action-researching teacher. The list makes interesting reading in the context of this discussion.

- I am willing to make improvements.
- I am healthily skeptical.
- I do not climb on board every change band wagon that comes along.
- I am selective and use discretion.
- I choose to explore only those changes that seem likely to meet the needs of my students.
- I treat each change as an intervention.
- I know that there is no perfect change and that I will have to modify my implementation efforts over time and as they happen.
- I need feedback. I need ongoing data to improve what I'm doing.
- I want to know that my improvements are working or not (so I can do better).

In conclusion, the number one task is to sustain the change process (as a learning journey) and your goal commitment over time. The second task is to be ready to amend and flexibly apply your change strategies—and be led by data in doing so. Is it actually the case that, in the synthesis of long-term commitment and alacrity of strategic response, the Development Culture has to absorb certain aspects of the Innovation Culture? Certainly, the balanced combination would seem to be strategic differentiation and experimentation (innovation) within a focused and shared goal agenda (development). As with students and the need to differentiate instructional responses to meet their individual and small-group learning needs, schools as learning organizations have to incorporate the right amount of flexibility, differentiation, and fleetness-of-foot.

ELEMENT 3

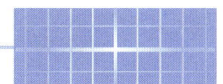

Follow-Through — Sustaining Changes Over Time

Follow-Through
Task 3: Reflecting on Element Three

Purpose: To summarize and synthesize what participants have learned about Element 3: Follow-Through.

Grouping: Work in triads.

Directions: In the light of this extended commentary, rewrite the "Going to Los Angeles" story so it more exactly fits how we should go about successfully making change happen over time. Share your rewritten versions with your Learning Team.

New version of "Going to Los Angeles":

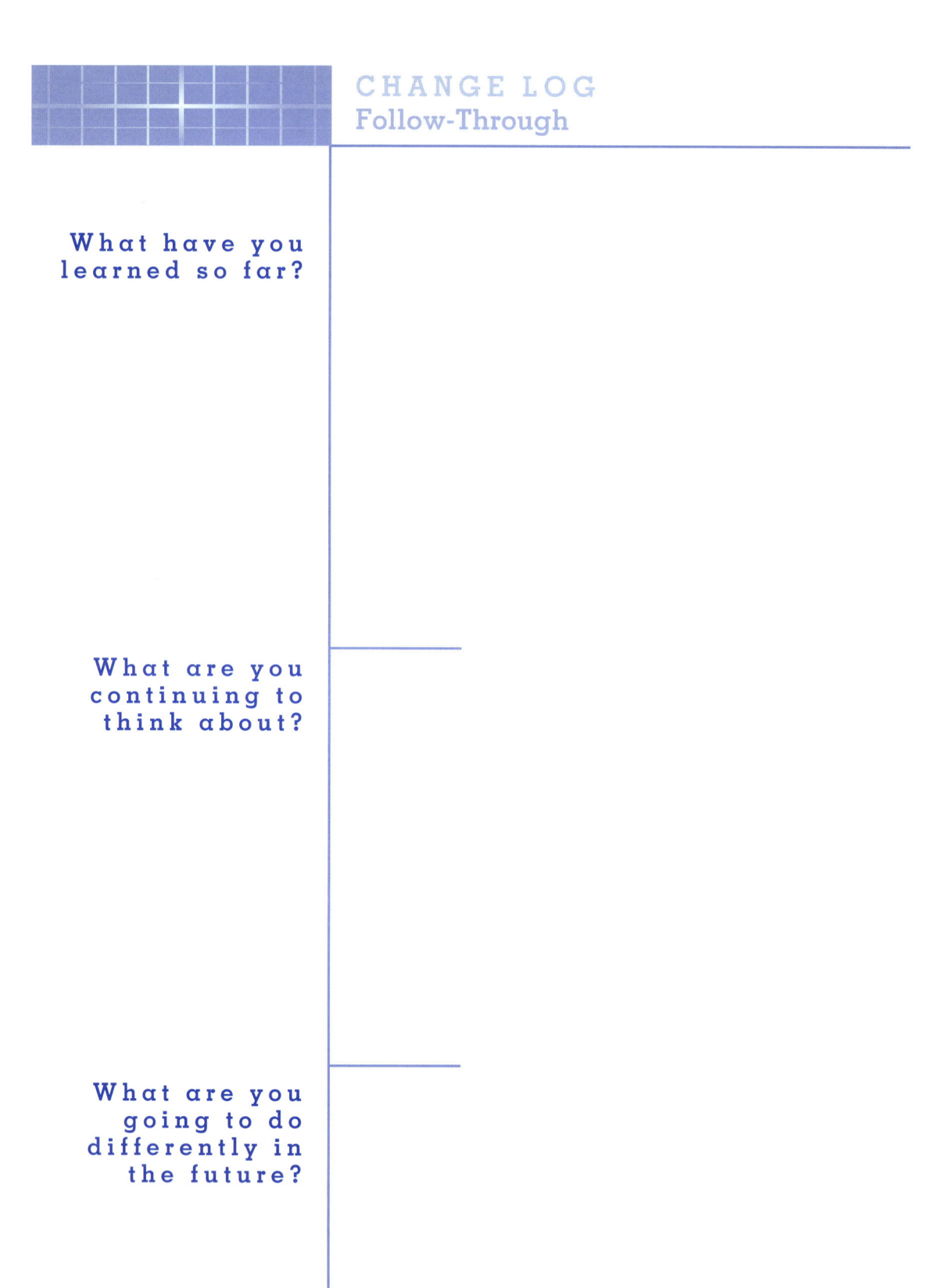

CHANGE LOG
Follow-Through

What have you learned so far?

What are you continuing to think about?

What are you going to do differently in the future?

ELEMENT 4
Grounding Our Change Efforts in Data

Overview

The model outlined in this workbook is data-driven. It entails the continuous use of data-based decision making to steer local school improvement efforts. What is unique about this model is that data not only inform but also drive the entire school improvement process. Essential skills, therefore, include data processing (the content of Workbook Three), learning from data, and the application of this learning to guide school improvement processes. One of these processes—action planning—is the fulcrum of the school improvement cycle. Action planning incorporates—and, indeed, is grounded in—data inputs and contains plans for data scrutiny of its output. Although data drive school improvement, different kinds of school improvement data are of interest to the different kinds of stakeholder groups that have a legitimate interest in school improvement issues. In terms of student, teacher, and school performance, educators tend to look for growth (development), while other groups look for comparative results (accountability). Both are legitimate stances and both have to be embraced by school improvement efforts.

Data Use is Foundational

In the model that is the basis for this workbook, data use is foundational. In fact, in everything you have read and worked on so far, a continuing theme has been the use of data to drive continuous school improvement.

- The Developing School is the Learning School because it relies on data to learn its way forward.

- The Innovation Culture is somewhat random and interest-based as opposed to the Development Culture that is systematically needs-based, data-driven.

- In the context of the bubble map, without data there is no discernment, no needs identification, and no prioritization.

- The "yes, but" teachers say, "Show us the data." In being appropriately cautious, they have twin considerations in mind. They have to know that the area being developed is, indeed, one of real need—as evidenced by internal data. They also have a need to know that the strategy being recommended has a successful track record and actually works—as evidenced by external data—before committing themselves to its implementation.

- Data help educators to get focused—by providing evidence of their needs and signaling where they should be concentrating their efforts.

- Data are the wherewithal for reflection; reflection leads to thoughtful, considered, more intentional actions.

CHAPTER 2

- Data are our friends; they get us beyond the randomness of hopes, hunches, and guesses and inform our choices and our decisions.

- When goals are databased, they are first triggered by our concerns (our intuitive anxieties), which, in turn, become our identified needs (when our concerns are substantiated in data).

- Internal and external data help us to identify what works—in terms of the best of the old and the best of the new—which can then be combined within a shared change agenda.

- Data are the basis of feedback—which can be used to guide our change efforts as they happen. We are given ongoing intelligence.

Data-Driven School Improvement

During the school improvement cycle there are four stages of data collection and these stages interact with the stages of school improvement—literally informing and, therefore, driving school improvement forward.

The four stages of data collection are as follows:

1. Collecting **Needs Assessment** data in order to understand needs, to establish priorities, and to set goals.

2. Collecting **Baseline** data on the current status in each goal area prior to implementation in order to measure growth at a later point in time.

3. Collecting **Up-close** data—during implementation—in order to carefully monitor progress over time and provide feedback to participants who can then make any necessary "in-flight" adjustments.

4. Collecting **Trend-line** data to determine how much and what kind of progress has been achieved in each of the goal areas.

Collecting up-close data is akin to formative/process evaluation and collecting trend-line data is like summative/product evaluation. When interconnected with the stages of the school improvement, the overall, integrated package—referred to below as the CREATE Cycle—becomes a model for data-driven school improvement.

ELEMENT 4

Grounding Our Change Efforts in Data

C.R.E.A.T.E.

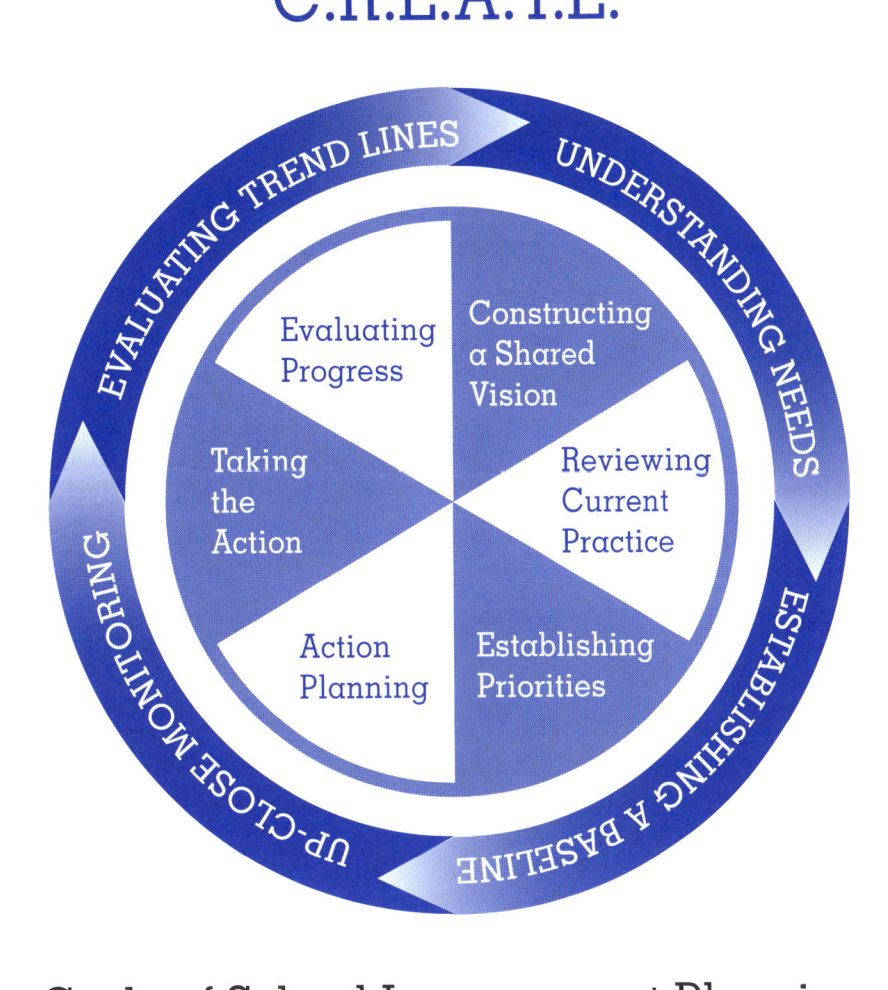

Cycle of School Improvement Planning

— Adapted from Holly and Southworth
Developing the School (1989)

The Central Role of Data in Action Planning

The author has argued that action plans are crucial in that they link planning with action. Action plans and the goals centered within them are grounded in needs assessment and baseline data. They can also look forward to the need for data collection to monitor and evaluate the plan's progress over time. Indeed, in action planning design, educators are encouraged to establish success criteria (student learning results or indicators of success, which, when accomplished, will demonstrate that the goals have been met) and data collection methods to use in mapping progress toward the success criteria. Only then, in what is referred to as the "1,4,5,2,3" design (which is described in detail in the second workbook in this series), does the author suggest that staff select their implementation strategies and support needs—including their staff development requirements. An example of the Action Planning Sheet is shown on the next page. It incorporates the "1, 4, 5, 2, 3" design which indicates the order in which steps (or columns) are completed.

CHAPTER 2

ACTION PLANNING SHEET

1 Goal Statement	2 Implementation Strategies

ELEMENT 4

Grounding Our Change Efforts in Data

3	4	5
Support Needs (including staff development)	**Success Criteria/ Specific Outcomes**	**Data Collection Methods**
	"Success will have been achieved when…"	Baseline: Up close: Trend line:

Calhoun (1999) echoes this approach. She says that teachers must look beyond data that are readily available (such as standardized test scores and grades) and do two things:

- Establish the specific student performances (the "success criteria") that they're trying to develop. In reading comprehension, for example:

    - Can students identify the main idea of a passage?

    - Can students explain how they determined the main idea?

    - Can students use multiple sources of information to form major ideas about a topic?

    - Can students identify the author's purpose?

- Regularly collect "up-close" data, data as close to the student performance as possible, to monitor the work being done to accomplish the goal—as it happens. For example, she says, work samples can be scrutinized on a weekly, bi-weekly, or monthly basis.

Indeed, in her 1999 published conversation with Dennis Sparks, Emily Calhoun describes the goal-based action planning process in terms very similar to the author's approach.

> Getting the goal...is a powerful beginning because it screens out some of the competing demands for time and attention and affects how resources will be invested.
>
> When a faculty selects a goal it believes will make the most difference in the education of students, it is setting the parameters for collective study and action. This focus on one powerful goal limits the amount of student learning data to collect, the amount of data to collect about what is currently happening in curriculum and instruction throughout the school, and the extensiveness of the study of the external knowledge base. It also makes possible the high quality staff development needed to support changes in instruction and the careful study of the implementation of strategies selected by the faculty. Even with one [goal], it's a big task.

ELEMENT 4

Grounding Our Change Efforts in Data

> There's a concept I call "seeing through and beyond," which means looking at all the changes that will be required. The faculty needs to look through the learning goal to the student performances the teachers want to see; teachers need to consider what successful goal attainment would look like for students. Then they need to determine what teacher behaviors in curriculum, instruction, and assessment are necessary to promote those student behaviors. Next, they must see right through the teacher behaviors to what the principal is doing and what the district office is doing. Having the goal helps us focus; then we push through it to the things that everyone must be doing to bring it into reality.

Both Calhoun and Fullan advise teachers to collect external data as part of the action planning process. Calhoun (1999), for instance, encourages teachers to reach out to the external knowledge base to interact with the ideas of others. Study time, she says, should be used to help faculty members select classroom strategies that are likely to yield increases in student achievement and learn how to use them to a high level of skill. Fullan (1996) argues that, in order to be able to select appropriate programs, educators need to have substantial knowledge of the available options—prior to making their choice. Moreover, he says, these same educators also need to have a good understanding of their existing approaches to learning in order to figure out how to integrate improvement initiatives into their work.

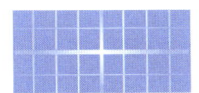

Grounding Our Change Efforts in Data
Task 1—Part 1: Action Planning

Purpose: To assess and improve current school improvement action planning efforts in the light of expert advice.

Grouping: Work individually.

67

CHAPTER 2

Directions: Write individual responses to the questions below.

1. Describe how school improvement action plans are established in your educational situation.

2. How well does the action planning process used in your situation match the advice given by experts?

ELEMENT 4

Grounding Our Change Efforts in Data

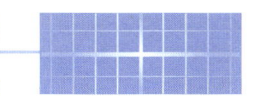

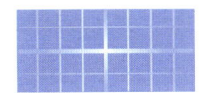

Grounding Our Change Efforts in Data
Task 1 — Part 2: Action Planning

Grouping: Meet with your Learning Team.

Group processing strategy: Use the Go Round and a Consensus Building strategy. Select a recorder to create a Team List.

Directions: Using the Go Round technique, share your individual answers with the members of your Learning Team, paying particular attention to any discrepancies in the responses of team members. Then, using the principle of "sufficient consensus," come to an agreement on a list of "action planning strengths" and "action planning challenges." Select a recorder to record these two lists on chart paper. Use this page of your workbook for note taking.

Action Planning Strengths	Action Planning Challenges

CHAPTER 2

Levels of Data Collection

At each of the stages of data collection outlined above, there are four levels of the local system at which to collect data:

- the student level
- the classroom/instructional level
- the school level
- the district level

While Joyce, Wolf, and Calhoun (1993) talk about three spheres of the local system (they collapse the student and classroom levels into one), this author finds it more useful to distinguish between individual student learning and teacher instructional levels.

Moreover, by combining the four stages of data collection (needs assessment data, baseline data, up-close data, and trend-line data) with the four levels of the local system, it becomes possible to create an interesting matrix or data-collection map (see the following page).

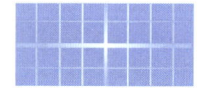

Grounding Our Change Efforts in Data ■ Task 2: Understanding the Interests of Stakeholder Groups

Purpose: To appreciate that various stakeholder groups have somewhat different—and legitimate—interests in data.

Grouping: Work in dyads or triads.

Directions: Using the data-collection matrix on the following page, plot where each stakeholder group is likely to have the most interest in data collection. Some cells of the matrix may be the targets of several stakeholder groups, while other cells may be under used. Some groups may have interest in more than one cell. Once you have completed this activity, respond to the questions following the matrix.

ELEMENT 4

Grounding Our Change Efforts in Data

Data Collection Matrix

Levels of Data Collection	Needs Assessment	Baseline	Up Close	Trend Line
Student				
Classroom/ Instructional				
School				
District				

STAGES OF DATA COLLECTION

1. Which cells are the targets of most interest and attention?

2. Which cells receive the least amount of interest and attention?

3. What have you learned by doing this exercise?

4. How would you interpret the significance of your answers to Questions 1 and 2?

5. What implications are there for the change process in your school district; in your school; and in your classroom?

ELEMENT 4

Grounding Our Change Efforts in Data

Grounding Our Change Efforts in Data
Task 3: Tracking Student Progress

Purpose: To undertake a vital planning exercise—how to track student progress on a school-wide basis—as part of a local response to the federal *No Child Left Behind* legislation.

Grouping: Work with your Learning Team.

Directions: This is a major Learning Team task. At the student level of a systemic approach to data collection, it is increasingly possible to track educational progress—student-by-student, disaggregated group-by-disaggregated group, class-by-class. In an era when the national intent is *No Child Left Behind*, as a team problem-solving activity, plan how this could be done for your school—by casting the data collection net as widely as possible.

Tracking Student Progress Plan

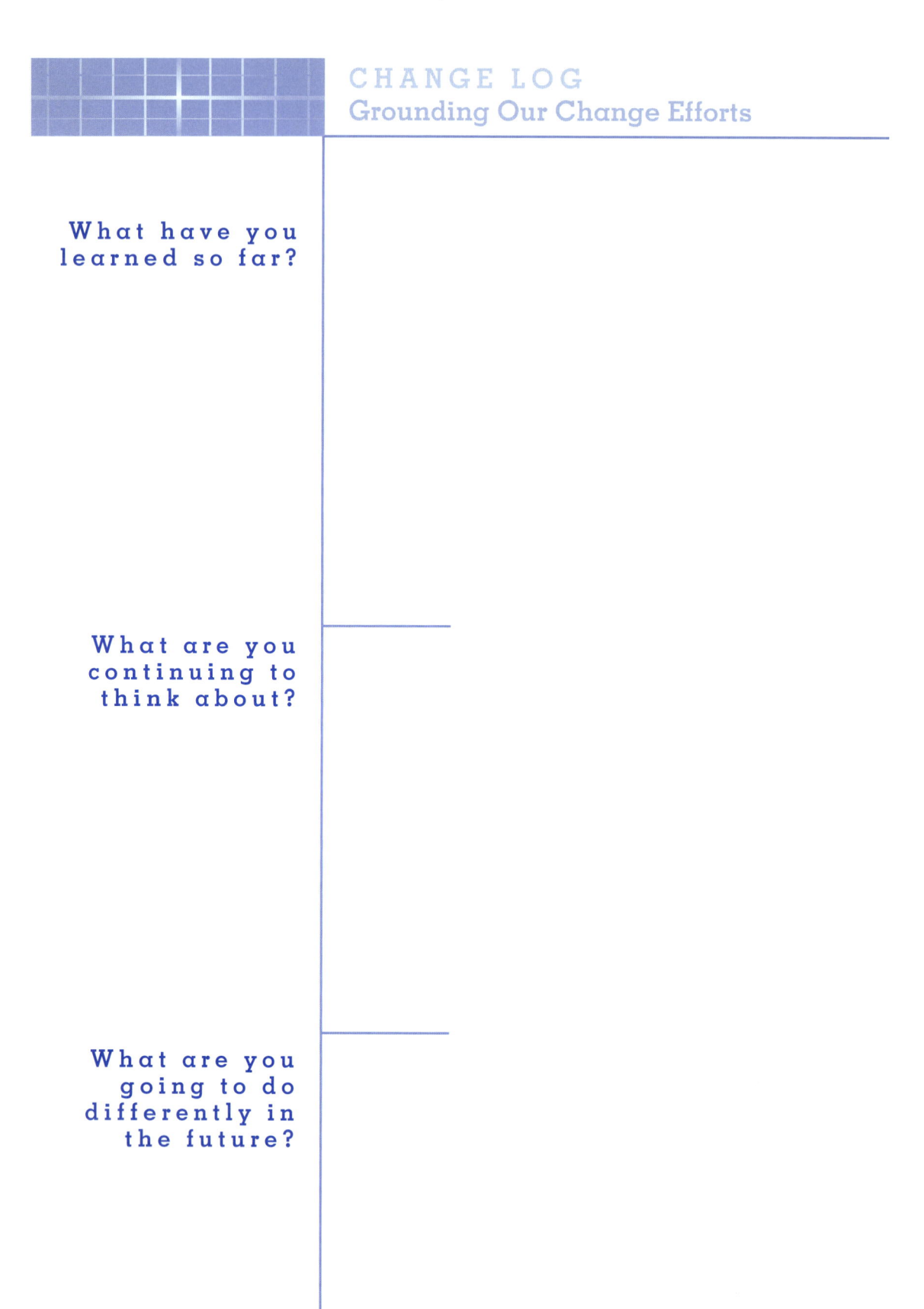

CHANGE LOG
Grounding Our Change Efforts

What have you learned so far?

What are you continuing to think about?

What are you going to do differently in the future?

Element 5

Data Show Our Progress

Overview

Data not only drive school improvement; as the means of progress monitoring, they help us stay on the chosen path. Indeed, data have a unique power. They can be used to confront us with our shortcomings, a process that is particularly powerful when we are shown where we are falling short against benchmarks that we ourselves helped to create in the first place. Data have the ability to pit us (and our efforts) against ourselves. Self-confrontation is the key activity here.

Committing to change requires both mind and heart; the intellectual acknowledgment of the need for change has to be matched by an emotional response that generates our commitment to actually doing something about it and wanting to succeed. It is data and their use that link the two sides of this equation: data show us the need and, in the process, convince us that the need demands our continuing attention. Then, when we act to address the need, we want to know that we're being successful—so we re-employ data to track our progress. When these new data reveal areas where we are falling short of our goals, we can be very specific and focused in our corrective interventions. To be shown that we are falling short of our agreed targets can provide just the spark we need to ignite our continued efforts and regenerate our determination to succeed.

Data Show Our Progress ■ Task 1: Understanding the Role of Data in School Improvement Efforts

Purpose: Participants learn the vital and continuing role played by data in school improvement efforts—that, on the path to school improvement, data tell us where we should be going and whether we're getting there or not.

LT

Grouping: Work with your Learning Team.

Directions: Joan Richardson (1996) wrote an article entitled, "If You Don't Know Where You're Going, How Will You Know When You Arrive?"

Please discuss the following two questions with your Learning Team members:

1. What thoughts does the title of Richardson's article evoke with your team?

CHAPTER 2

2. How can using data help us respond to Richardson's challenge?

Let Data be Our Guide

According to John Gardner (1963):

> Renewal is not just innovation and change. It is also the process of bringing the results of change into line with our purposes.

Data keep us honest. They tell us about our accomplishments and to what extent the results of our actions are aligned with our hopes and aspirations. They also indicate to us whether (and where) we are falling short of our ambitions. Data have the ability to show us the gaps between our desired state and the current reality. Gap analysis, as it is called, involves the examination of our data to search for these important performance gaps between our long-term vision and our everyday practice.

Vision—incorporating core beliefs and values—has to be in place in order to have something to assess our progress against. Again, in John Gardner's words:

> Particularly important to a society's continuity are its long-term purposes and values. These purposes and values also evolve in the long run; but by being relatively durable, they enable a society to absorb change without losing its distinctive character and style. They do much to determine the direction of change. They insure that a society will not be buffeted in all directions by every wind that blows.

Members of a middle school faculty in Kentucky echoed these sentiments by concluding: We used to change for the sake of change but now we're changing with a purpose and that's much more powerful.

ELEMENT 5
Data Show Our Progress

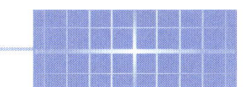

As part of their visioning process, after an extensive review of the external knowledge base and the burgeoning literature on middle schools, the same staff created a set of Essential Learnings. Our students, they agreed, will demonstrate the ability to

- think critically, creatively, and independently
- work collaboratively with peers
- solve problems
- take responsibility for their learning
- regulate and evaluate their performance
- communicate effectively
- assume leadership roles
- apply knowledge to real-life situations

Having created this list, the faculty members realized that these Essential Learnings would have to be the lodestone for their school and its continuing improvement. Their first step, therefore, was to create some data to guide their actions. A brief staff survey was constructed and distributed to all staff teams (see the following page). The returns were then analyzed and staff dialogue conducted concerning the results. The purpose of producing this data (survey responses and opinions elicited during the conversations) was to be able to gauge the current status of each of the Essential Learnings. The outcome of the exercise was to obtain a general picture of which Essential Learnings were already strengths and which could be deemed deficiencies—thus becoming priorities for development. As a result of canvassing staff opinion in this way, the fourth Essential Learning (students taking responsibility for their learning) became their new school improvement goal.

CHAPTER 2

STAFF SURVEY

Students on our team can demonstrate the ability to…

	Strongly Agree	Agree	No Opinion	Disagree	Strongly Disagree
■ think critically, creatively, and independently	☐	☐	☐	☐	☐
■ work collaboratively with peers	☐	☐	☐	☐	☐
■ solve problems	☐	☐	☐	☐	☐
■ take responsibility for their learning	☐	☐	☐	☐	☐
■ regulate and evaluate their performance	☐	☐	☐	☐	☐
■ communicate effectively	☐	☐	☐	☐	☐
■ assume leadership roles	☐	☐	☐	☐	☐
■ apply knowledge to real-life situations	☐	☐	☐	☐	☐

During the process of needs identification followed by goal selection, the staff came to realize the overall importance of their Essential Learnings. They understood the following:

- ■ The Essential Learnings were good for five to ten years—as a guide to curriculum and instructional decision making.

- ■ They would have to be used, honored, and celebrated on a daily basis and infused in everything done by staff members.

- ■ Adult modeling—the so-called hidden curriculum—would be vital.

- ■ Annual school goals and action plans would have to be centered on progress toward the Essential Learnings.

- ■ More baseline data were required—to provide more depth of information concerning the current status of each of the Essential Learnings.

ELEMENT 5

Data Show Our Progress

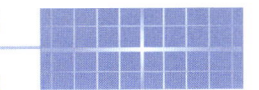

- Thereafter, annual assessments would have to be conducted in all the areas to chart the extent of progress made.

- Ongoing teacher and team action research would be required to chart progress as it happened—in order to be able to make smart, collaborative, and ongoing instructional adjustments.

- There was an obvious connection with the district's school-to-work initiative, influenced, itself, by the recent publication of the SCANS Report, and the need for students to acquire life skills and life-long learning standards.

- Above all, the Essential Learnings would have to be used to redesign daily instructional and assessment practices. There would have to be a shift to more criterion-based, performance-based assessment, including student self-assessment.

Having worked with this staff during what was an intensive and pivotal stage in their school's development, this author came to understand the central importance of Essential Learnings. In an article entitled, "Why Essential Learnings?" (Holly, 1995), the reasons for their significance are listed as follows:

- They constitute the iron hoop around the barrel that holds together the whole local system. In a system with Handy's "simultaneous tight-loose properties," they represent the tightness; the looseness comes in how they are used on a daily basis [Handy, 1984].

- They are cross-curricular and inter-disciplinary. They have to permeate and be infused in everything we do. They constitute the Horizontal Curriculum.

- They are Essential Learnings for all students. They will be a constant challenge for some students and a launching pad for others.

- They provide curricular clarity, consistency, and continuity and are the basis for better communication.

- They are best seen as a local system's long-term learning goals and, as such, should guide individual classroom practice (what to teach, how to learn, and how to demonstrate successful learning experiences).

- Moreover, they foster the understanding at the individual teacher level that working on them in the classroom constitutes a teacher's personal contribution to the implementation of the school improvement plan.

- They provide a vital link with the community.

- They embrace the social, behavioral, emotional, and intellectual aspects of learning.

CHAPTER 2

- They are the umbrella under which many school improvement data-based decisions can be clustered.

- It is a central task of the school principal and other members of the system leadership team to keep the importance of achieving the Essential Learnings at the top of every agenda, every change conversation, every meeting, and every planning session.

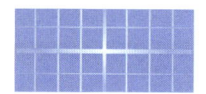

Data Show Our Progress ▪ Task 2: Creating Your Local Version of Essential Learnings

<u>Purpose:</u> To learn the importance of establishing Essential Learnings and their centrality in school improvements efforts.

LT

<u>Grouping:</u> Work with your Learning Team.

<u>Directions:</u> Working in your Learning Team, enter your local version of Essential Learnings and then answer the questions in the space provided on the following page.

Our Local Version of Essential Learnings

ELEMENT 5

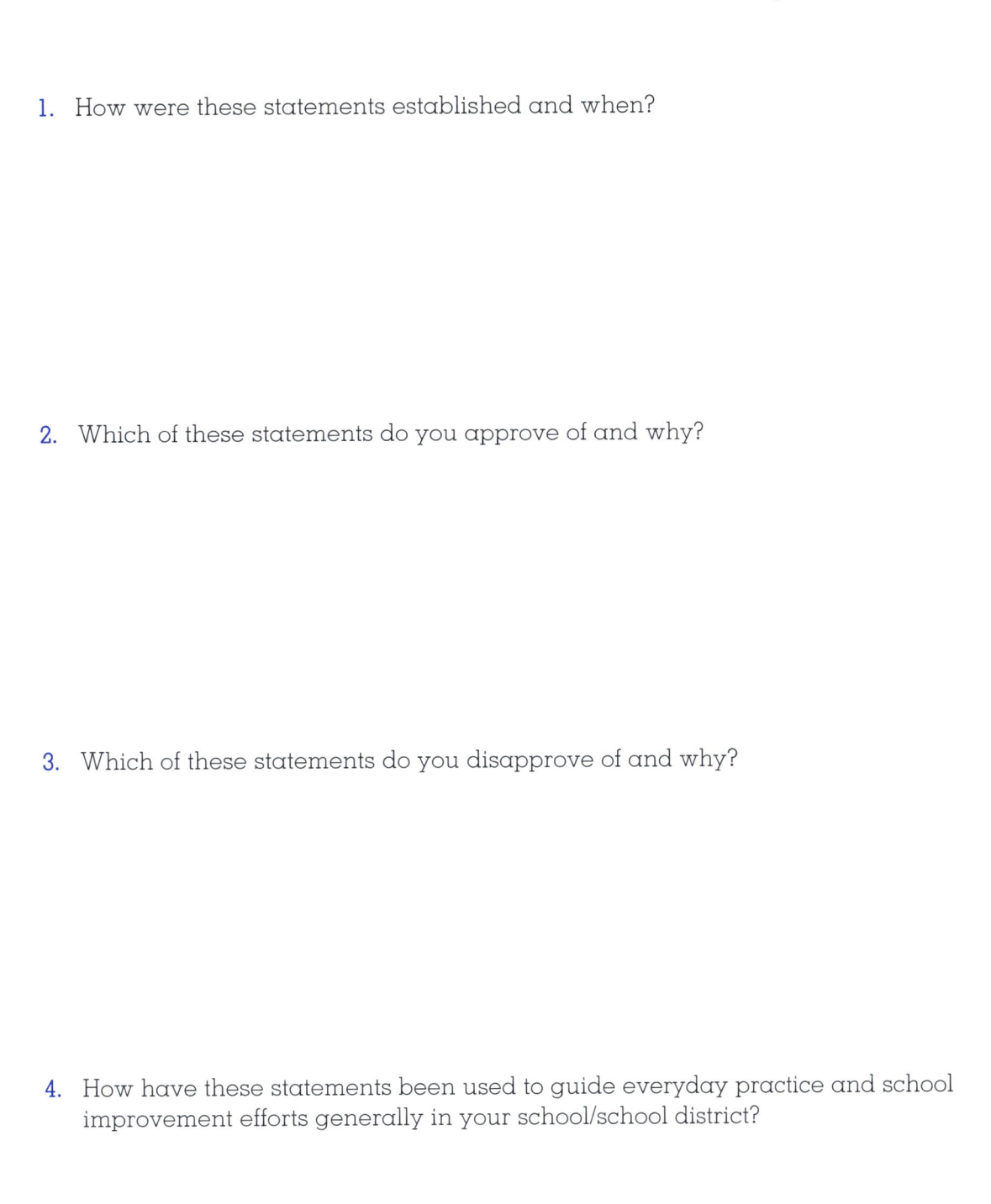

Data Show Our Progress

1. How were these statements established and when?

2. Which of these statements do you approve of and why?

3. Which of these statements do you disapprove of and why?

4. How have these statements been used to guide everyday practice and school improvement efforts generally in your school/school district?

CHAPTER 2

Data Show Our Progress
Task 3: Constructing a Needs Assessment Tool

Purpose: To construct an instrument that can be used to assess the extent to which Essential Learnings are being applied in the participants' school(s).

Grouping: Work with your Learning Team.

Directions: Using your local version of Essential Learnings (refer to Task 2), work as a team to construct a needs assessment tool that will help you find out where you are in your school(s) vis-à-vis these Essential Learnings. You may want to review the staff survey form that was referenced earlier in this section.

Note: The next task asks you to apply this instrument across your school(s)

Our Needs Assessment Tool

ELEMENT 5
Data Show Our Progress

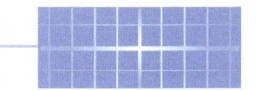

Keepers of the Vision

Hessel and Holloway (2002) have recently underlined the important role of leadership concerning a system's vision and its accomplishment over time.

> The effective school leader works for continuous school improvement achieved through a cyclical, or recursive, process in which the school's vision, mission, and strategic plans are developed, implemented, monitored, evaluated, and revised. The leader understands the change process, and knows that part of that process is the systematic examination of assumptions, beliefs, and practices and of the school culture and climate. The process includes also identifying, clarifying, and addressing barriers to achieving the school's vision. The effective leader assures that the process is inclusive, involving all stakeholders...He or she uses a variety of information sources, including assessment and demographic data, to make decisions.
>
> As plans to implement the vision are put into action, the school leader must assure that these plans are monitored from the beginning and evaluated over time. The school leader systematically collects and analyzes data on the school progress towards realizing the vision. This monitoring and evaluation must be tied directly to objectives and strategies. Demonstrating a clear understanding of the link between effective teaching and student learning, the school leader also regularly collects data on both student achievement and teacher performance.... Monitoring and evaluating the vision...is an ongoing inclusive process. It includes informal and formal methods. Stakeholders are afforded opportunities, through such strategies as surveys or questionnaires, open forums, and dialogues, to indicate how well they believe the implementation plan is working. The accomplished school leader invites the appropriate stakeholders to analyze and review this information during the year.

CHAPTER 2

As Keepers of the Vision, school leaders have to commit to tracking—in data—its implementation over time. This is all the more important in the kind of system suggested by Handy (1989) and Mintzberg (1994) where a common vision is used to guide all school improvement efforts but, working within the vision, participants can use different and/or multiple strategies to achieve success.

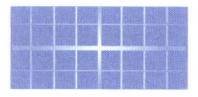

Data Show Our Progress
Task 4: Identifying Local Keepers of the Vision

Purpose: To review who plays the role of "Keepers of the Vision" in participants' school(s) and how effectively the role is played.

Grouping: Work individually, and then with your Learning Team members.

Group process strategy: Use the Go Round method for sharing.

Directions: Answer the following questions individually and then pool your responses by completing a Go Round with your team.

1. Who fulfills the role of Keepers of the Vision in your educational situation?

2. What advice would you give them in order to improve how they perform this role?

ELEMENT 5
Data Show Our Progress

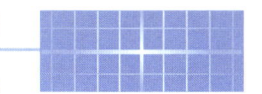

The Power of Gap Analysis

The crucial task of gap analysis—the identification and explanation of the discrepancies between our desired state, our vision, and our current reality—can only be achieved through the use of relevant data. It is data that illuminate the nature and extent of our discrepancies and performance gaps. There is, however, more to this. Data perform a crucial role beyond the first step of illumination. Data challenge our assumptions and our beliefs and challenge us in our comfort zones. Data can be discomforting. Through the activation of "cognitive dissonance" (Festinger, 1954), we are shown that what Argyris and Schon (1978) call our espoused theories (our desired state, our vision) are not matched by our theories-in-use (that guide and determine our everyday actions). Simply put, we are shown that our behaviors do not match our values and beliefs. We are hooked by our own incongruity.

In the experience of this author, there is something "neutral" about data that cannot be denied. This is not merely an argument about the technical adequacy of data—however important and contributory that may be. It's about how we receive data. Data come from outside us; they are objective and surprisingly non-threatening—they speak to how things are rather than to judgments that could be made about them. Because of our receptiveness to data, they challenge us, provoke us, and stimulate us in ways other media cannot seem to do.

Sagor (1993) reminds us of cognitive dissonance theory and its potential role in the change process. Cognitive dissonance theory, he says, argues that when our attitudes and beliefs and our behaviors are in conflict we will tend to experience heightened anxiety and stress. Given that there is a natural need for stress reduction, according to Sagor, there are three ways forward: encourage individuals to engage in new behaviors; ensure, through positive reinforcement, that the new behaviors engender ample feelings of personal success and efficacy; and embark on a deliberate and continuous focus on data that show both that positive changes are required and that progress is occurring. According to Peter Senge (1990), such a process will produce enough "creative tension" to motivate those involved to reduce the gap between where we are and where we know we ought to be.

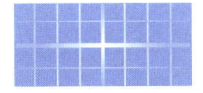

Data Show Our Progress
Task 5: Completing a Gap Analysis

<u>Purpose:</u> To learn by doing—to learn how a gap analysis works by using the technique to discover discrepancies between the desired state and the current reality in the participants' schools.

CHAPTER 2

<u>Grouping:</u> Work individually first, and then with your Learning Team.

<u>Group process strategy:</u> Use a Consensus Building strategy.

<u>Directions:</u> This is another major task for your team. It involves a gap analysis of the main themes found in this element so far. You are asked to look at each item of the instrument below and rate it in two ways: **Importance** means how important this item should be to us and **Current Status** means the level of importance each item *is currently receiving*. Each rating is on a 1-5 scale with 1 being "not very important" and 5 being "very important." After completing the instrument, the next step is to subtract the **Current Status** score from the **Importance** score—for each item—to obtain the size of the discrepancy (**the Gap Size**). The higher the discrepancy score, the larger the gap between what *should be* the case and what *is* the case. After you have completed this task individually, meet with your Learning Team colleagues to come up with a consensus version. This is also an appropriate task for the faculty, in general, to complete.

In our school:	Importance	Current Status	Gap Size
We know where we're going.			
We use data to tell us how far we've progressed.			
We use data to tell us if our vision is being achieved.			
We have a strong vision that is pointing us forward.			
Our change efforts are purposeful.			
Essential Learnings guide our classroom efforts.			
Our school leaders serve as "Keepers of the Vision."			

ELEMENT 5
Data Show Our Progress

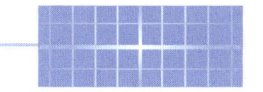

According to Sagor (1993):

> Alienated school families will continue to teach as they've always taught. They will continue to organize schools as they have always been organized, unless, or until, they have reason to believe that changes in process will produce changes in their results. Data on student performance can create the requisite dissonance to cause the faculty to reexamine their attitudes and roles. Likewise, data on their own accomplishments will inspire students to seek out more successful experiences. The task for school reformers is to get both students and teachers involved with meaningful and thought-provoking data on student and school performance.

These comments remind this author of a research project that he read about several years ago. The project involved disaffected youth in schools. Videotapes were made of their classroom behaviors and then played back to them in one-on-one sessions with skilled facilitators. They had to be individual sessions because their negative attitudes might have actually worsened if they'd been questioned in front of their reference group—their equally disaffected peers. When confronted with the reality of their videotaped behaviors, at first they were affronted, angry, and full of rebuttals—they said things like, "that's not me" and "I wouldn't behave like that."

This denial stage was followed by a stage characterized by making excuses. Typical comments were, "We were only doing that for the camera," "we don't ordinarily behave like that," and "one of my friends made me do that." After much persistence on the part of the facilitator, an important third stage was reached. This was where the process known as "de-centering" really began to take effect and the students became reflective observers of their own behavior. Their filmed behavior was now data: it enabled them to enter the "neutral zone." Their behavior (as data) was outside them, not quite part of them, and they could become dispassionate "students" of what they were viewing. They became analytical and were able to cite reasons why these "other" students might have behaved in these ways. Apparently, this same approach can work equally well for students and adults.

CHAPTER 2

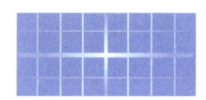

Data Show Our Progress
Task 6: Reflecting on De-Centering

<u>Purpose:</u> To reflect on—and appreciate the importance of—the approach known as "de-centering."

<u>Grouping:</u> Work with your Learning Team.

<u>Group process strategy:</u> Use the Circle configuration. You will need to select a recorder.

<u>Directions:</u> In your Learning Team (this is an ideal time to arrange yourselves in the Circle Configuration), respond to these three questions and have a recorder summarize your reflections:

1. How does the approach known as "de-centering" work?

ELEMENT 5
Data Show Our Progress

2. Why is it so powerful?

3. What are some other possible applications of the "de-centering" approach in the school improvement process?

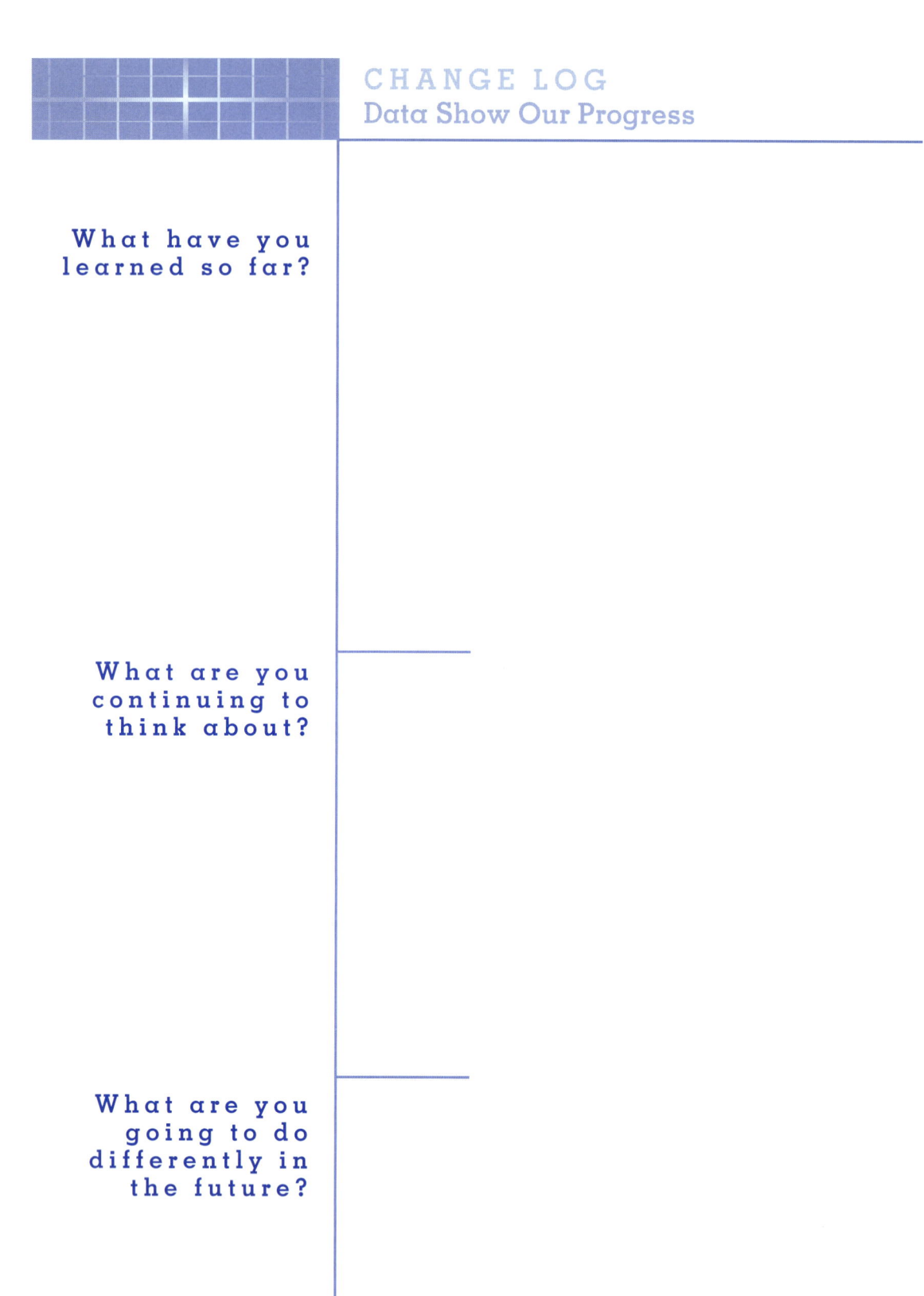

CHANGE LOG
Data Show Our Progress

What have you learned so far?

What are you continuing to think about?

What are you going to do differently in the future?

Element 6

Continuous Improvement in the Self-Renewing School

Overview

The model introduced in this workbook—data-driven continuous school improvement—is the engine for the self-renewing school. Shared decision making and data processing both contribute to **institutional competence**—the capacity to grow from the inside while being educated from the outside. It's a case of organic growth as opposed to mechanistic change.

> In the production of a mechanism the constructive energy lies outside it, and adds discrete parts to discrete parts. The case is far different for a living organism which grows by its own impulse towards self-development. This impulse can be stimulated and guided from outside the organism, and it can also be killed. But for all your stimulation and guidance the creative impulse towards growth comes from within, and is intensely characteristic of the individual....What I am now insisting is that the principle of progress is from within: the discovery is made by ourselves, the discipline is self-discipline, and the fruition is the outcome of our own initiative.

This classic passage is from Alfred North Whitehead's *The Aims of Education* (first published in 1932). His words go to the essence of this element. Data inform, educate, and create new knowledge from the outside, but the learning process—that is self-development—has to be generated from the inside. Both Whitehead (1932) and Handy (1989) equate learning and change; the processes are one and the same, they say. Equally, they argue, the learning/change process is the same at whatever system level. The components and principles of student learning, therefore, are the same as those of organizational learning. According to Whitehead, the rhythmic, cyclical process of growth and learning should always contain both (internally-generated) freedom and (externally-generated) discipline. In a growing organism, he says, the "the ordered acquirement of knowledge" is the "natural food for a developing intelligence." In what amounts to a symbiotic relationship, says Whitehead, each should leaven the other in the natural sway of development. It is exactly the same in the Learning School that is the (Self-)Developing and Self-Renewing School.

Broad-based staff involvement in using data to make change decisions helps create a shared agenda for continuous school improvement. But it goes deeper than this. As a result of the depth of involvement, staff ownership, commitment, and collegiality are all enhanced. Yet it goes deeper than this. As Holly and Southworth (1989) and Joyce, Wolf, and Calhoun (1993) have maintained, the lodging of internal control within the organization is fundamental to the creation of the Learning School that is the Developing School and the Self-Renewing School. In the Learning School, while guided from the outside, change is generated from the inside. It is a case, says Holly (1994), of internalization (which involves internal commitment and the generation of change from within) educated and tempered by externalization (which involves rising to the challenges presented by external demands and pressures).

According to John Gardner (1963) in his seminal text entitled *Self-Renewal*, the self-renewing organization is a system that provides for its own continuous renewal. It embraces continuity and change ("something old, something new"). In a world buffeted by change, says Gardner, the only way to conserve is by innovating. The only stability possible is stability in motion. And this stability in motion entails the establishment of an internal capacity for generating continuous improvement—what Gardner calls "self development." The constituent elements of self-development, he says, are the discovery of talent, self-knowledge, the courage to fail, love (defined as mutually fruitful relations with others), and motivation. He also emphasizes the importance of tough-minded optimism, staying power, and the cohesiveness that comes with shared values—themes that echo throughout this workbook. In *The Developing School*, Holly and Southworth (1989) explored the application of Gardner's ideas to the school as a learning organization. The Learning School, they said, learns its way forward.

> Such an organization has the capacity to learn: how to develop from the inside; how to develop internally by responding to demands from the outside; and how to anticipate the shape of the future....The Learning School, if it is to be adaptive, self-balancing, and self-managing, needs enough autonomy for it to be sufficiently self-determining.

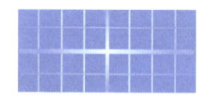

The Self-Renewing School
Task 1: Applying the Characteristics of a Learning School

Purpose: To apply the properties of a Learning School in an assessment of the participants' local situation.

Grouping: Work in pairs (dyads) or triads.

ELEMENT 6

Continuous Improvement in the Self-Renewing School

Directions: Discuss the following questions with your Learning Team colleagues:

1. In what ways does your educational organization match up with the characteristics contained in this description of the Learning School? What are the missing elements?

2. In your situation, is the Learning School a feasible concept? Why or why not?

Institutional Competence and the Self-Renewing School

According to Timar and Kirp (1987):

> Reform is most needed where learning takes place—in the individual schools, in the classroom, and in the interaction between teacher and student. As businesses world-wide have learned, problems can best be solved at the lowest level of operation. While structures are needed, bureaucracies tend to focus on rules and regulations rather than results, thus stifling initiative. Therefore, we believe that school governance should be retained at the local level.

Furthermore, they argue, in order to achieve success at the local level, what is needed is "institutional competence," which is the school's internal capacity for generating growth and renewal. It is epitomized, said Holly and Southworth (1989), by the process of school improvement planning. To those in the UK who claimed that school development planning was yet another change with which to deal, this author (1990) commented:

CHAPTER 2

> It is *the* initiative, not yet another initiative; it's not part of the problem (of innovation overload), it's part of the solution. It's a case of developing the institutional competence to handle change effectively.

The point is that some process changes have to be embedded within the school's internal capacity in order to be able to process—and sift and filter—all the content changes that come along. Some process changes are pre-ordinate, and improvement planning is one of them.

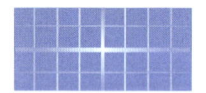

The Self-Renewing School ■ Task 2: Identifying Local External Requirements and Internal Needs

<u>Purpose:</u> To understand the tension between external requirements and internal needs.

<u>Grouping:</u> Work individually and then with your Learning Team to create Team Lists.

<u>Directions:</u> Make two lists below: one of the external requirements currently being asked of your school and another of the internal needs that have been identified and are awaiting attention. First brainstorm individually, then combine your ideas into one composite list for the Learning Team.

External Requirements   Internal Needs

ELEMENT 6

Continuous Improvement in the Self-Renewing School

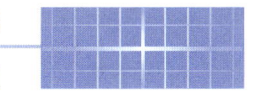

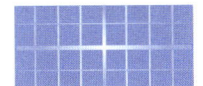

The Self-Renewing School ■ Task 3: Attending to Both External Requirements and Internal Needs

Purpose: To understand the importance of "internalizing the external."

Grouping: Work with your Learning Team.

Directions: Reflect as a Learning Team upon this question:

Looking at the two lists generated in Task 2, how can a school like your own attend to both internal needs and external requirements and still retain the vital characteristics of the Self-Renewing School?

The Self-Renewing School

Joyce, Wolf, and Calhoun (1993) have explored the concept of the self-renewing school or school district. Task one, they say, is to embed a capacity for change inside the organization. Specialists in organizational behavior, leadership, change, training, and action research show a remarkable degree of agreement concerning the centrality of this task. Joyce et al. continue:

> A self-renewing school is inquiry-oriented. School staff examine evidence before they adopt initiatives, and they examine evidence when changes are made. Teachers make adjustments as they assess the impact of the changes. Life in the organization is conducted in an experimental mode. Thus, in a self-renewing school, everyone engages in action research on a continuous basis, keeping the central mission at the heart of the operation.

The central mission, they say, is the enhancement of student learning. Indeed, the Learning School (that is also the self-renewing school) attends to the question of learning on three levels. Student learning is the central mission, which, in turn, is supported by teacher learning and organizational learning. Action research is the vehicle to achieve all three levels of endeavor. As Joyce, Wolf, and Calhoun explain:

> By engaging in collegial action research, the members clarify areas needing attention; select initiatives on the basis of the best available evidence;

> and, by tracking implementation, determine effects on students. Staff members then adjust initiatives or select new ones.
>
> If the organization recreates itself into a healthy learning community where working together, studying together, and growing together have been planned into the system as a way of life, work in schools becomes synonymous with lifelong learning.

In such a learning community, say the same authors, there is more democratic access to knowledge. Everyone becomes knowledgeable about group decision making, options for staff development, collegial implementation of curriculum, action research for school improvement, and change as a personal and organizational process.

In a second publication, Joyce and Calhoun (1995) further explore school renewal as "an inquiry, not a formula." Their intent, they repeat, is to make schools learning communities for students and staff. Moreover, they say:

> Schools have previously been hampered by no time in the workday for collegial inquiry, no structures for democratic decision making, a shortage of information, and the absence of a pervasive staff development system.
>
> What is now envisioned is a quantum leap toward the creation of a setting where inquiry is normal and the conditions of the workplace support continuous, collegial inquiry.
>
> The process is school-based, involves the total faculty, builds community, serves to increase student learning through the study of instruction and curriculum, and seeks to provide a nurturant organization through collective study of the health of the school.

ELEMENT 6
Continuous Improvement in the Self-Renewing School

Based on these assertions, these same authors propose six hypotheses to guide thoughtful action in support of school renewal:

- Building in time for collective inquiry will increase school improvement activity.

- Active democracy and collective inquiry create the structural conditions for school improvement.

- Studying the learning environment will increase inquiry into ways of helping students learn better.

- Connecting the faculty to the knowledge base on teaching and learning will generate more meaningful initiatives.

- Staff development, structured as an inquiry into curriculum and instruction, will provide synergy and result in initiatives that have greater student effects.

- Working in small groups, with teachers sharing responsibility for their own learning and for helping one another, a faculty can become a nurturant unit.

Echoing Schaefer (1967), Joyce et al. constantly revisit the theme of the school as a center of collaborative inquiry:

> Inquiry involves collecting, analyzing, and reflecting on data. In an odd sense, our schools have been both information-rich and information impoverished. That is, while much information-gathering goes on, schools have lacked the reflective, experimental qualities that make assessment of learning lead to the study of ways to improve it....Every school has large quantities of data available for collective inquiry. Faculties may begin by using information such as grades and referrals, then collect new data, such as how often and how well students are comprehending and composing. But the inquiry doesn't necessarily stop here. At times, faculty members will want to collect data about students' feelings—for example, how students feel about their sense of independence and their developing concepts of themselves as effective human beings. These perceptual and attitudinal data can enrich a faculty's understanding of student behaviors and responses to the learning opportunities provided.

CHAPTER 2

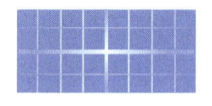

The Self-Renewing School ■ Task 4: Using the Properties of a Self-Renewing School to Complete a Local Assessment

<u>Purpose:</u> To use the properties of a self-renewing school to assess current performance.

<u>Grouping:</u> Work individually and then meet with your Learning Team to create Team Lists.

<u>Directions:</u> On your own, respond to each of these statements in terms of a 5-point scale: Always (5); Often (4); Sometimes (3); Seldom (2); Never (1).

In our school and/or school district:

_____ Time is set aside for collective inquiry.

_____ A Leadership Team coordinates all school improvement activities.

_____ We study the learning environment.

_____ We are connected to the external knowledge base.

_____ Staff development opportunities encourage collaborative inquiry.

_____ We are encouraged to work in small learning groups.

As a Learning Team, share your responses; discuss what **strengths** and **challenges** are indicated, and compile two lists below. Then, discuss what implications the strengths and challenges have for continuous improvement in your school.

Strengths	Challenges

ELEMENT 6

Continuous Improvement in the Self-Renewing School

In the Learning School:

- Fostering student learning is the vision and the daily business of the organization.

- Supporting and encouraging teacher learning and experimentation, by applying everything we know from adult learning theory, is the next priority.

- The school faculty, staff, and community members work together and learn their way forward. By so doing they constitute a self-renewing, learning organization.

This author (1990) has also argued that the self-renewing school rests on three interconnected building blocks: shared decision making, action research, and school improvement planning. This integrated package is referred to as "school-based development" (see the diagram below) and some key questions have been designed for educators to answer about their schools.

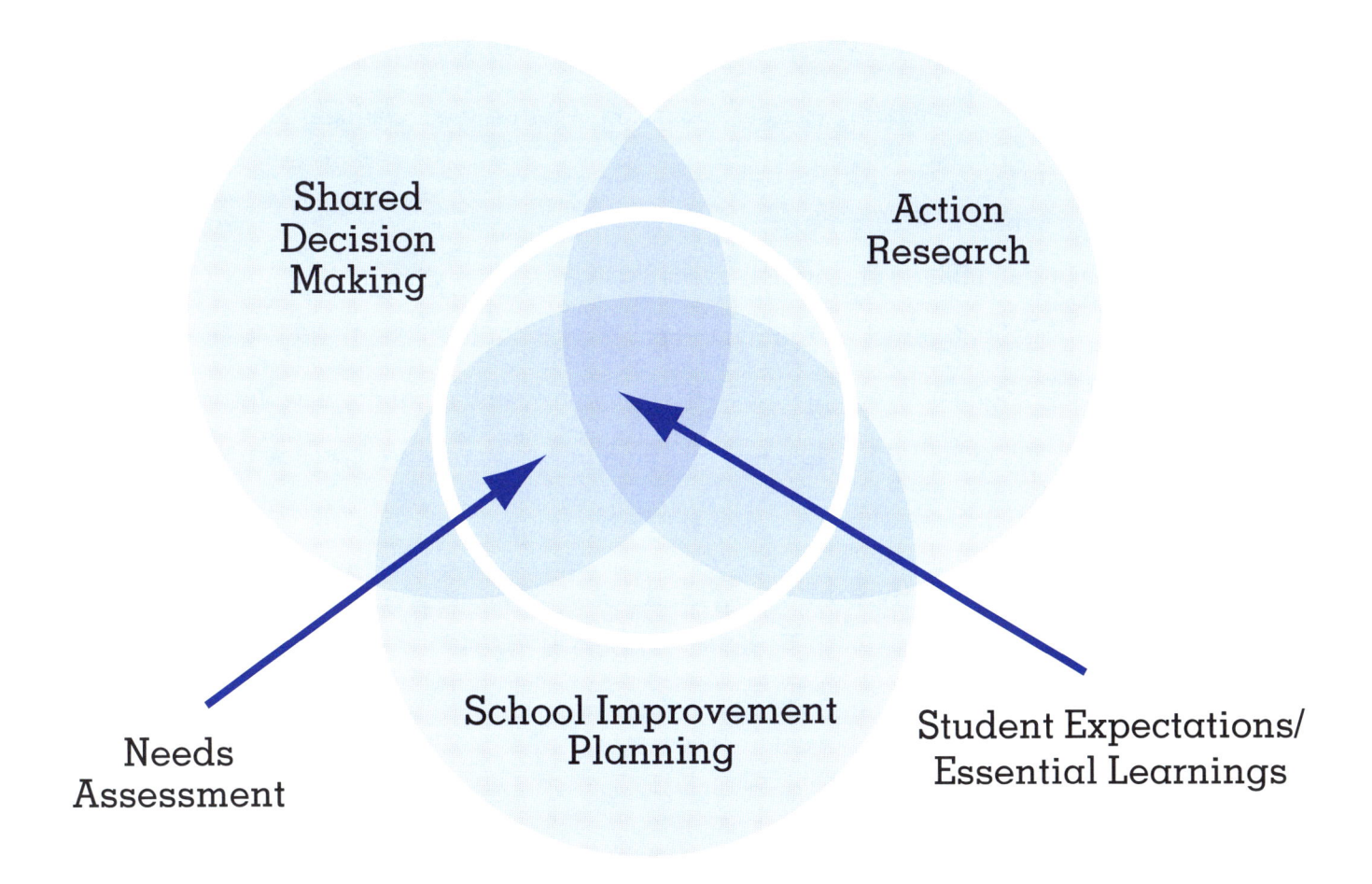

Shared Decision Making

Action Research

Needs Assessment

School Improvement Planning

Student Expectations/ Essential Learnings

CHAPTER 2

Shared Decision Making

- Is everyone involved—beyond the Site Council? How?
- Are parents getting involved? In what ways?
- Have Action Teams been formed?
- Is shared decision making being used to deal with significant issues?

Action Research

- Is data collection happening as a norm?
- Is it being used to inform decision making?
- Are needs being identified which can be translated into goals for school improvement planning?
- Is action research being used to reach and mobilize the classroom level?

School Improvement Planning

- Is the school improvement plan needs based and data-driven?
- Does the Site Council coordinate the production of the school improvement plan?
- Is the school improvement plan revised annually in the light of new data?
- Is the plan compatible with state and federal requirements?

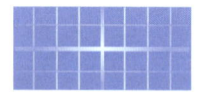

The Self-Renewing School ■ Task 5: Evaluating the Performance of Your School System

Purpose: To understand that the self-renewing school incorporates action research, shared decision making, and school improvement planning as building blocks for its continuing growth.

Grouping: Work individually, and then meet with your Learning Team.

ELEMENT 6

Continuous Improvement in the Self-Renewing School

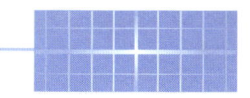

Group process strategy: Use a Consensus Building strategy.

Directions: Using these same twelve questions, evaluate the performance of your school system on a 1-5 scale (1 being "low" and 5 being "high") for each item. Complete this stage individually and then, in your Learning Team, agree, by consensus, on which items scored lowest and are in the most need of attention. Also discuss how your school system might go about dealing with these needs.

Shared Decision Making

____ Is everyone involved—beyond the Site Council? How?

____ Are parents getting involved? In what ways?

____ Have Action Teams been formed?

____ Is shared decision making being used to deal with significant issues?

Action Research

____ Is data collection happening as a norm?

____ Is it being used to inform decision making?

____ Are needs being identified which can be translated into goals for school improvement planning?

____ Is action research being used to reach and mobilize the classroom level?

School Improvement Planning

____ Is the school improvement plan needs based and data-driven?

____ Does the Site Council coordinate the production of the school improvement plan?

____ Is the school improvement plan revised annually in the light of new data?

____ Is the plan compatible with state and federal requirements?

Shared Decision Making

The second workbook in this series explores how to connect the data-driven and continuous aspects of school improvement. This is the place, however, to acknowledge the crucial role played by shared decision making.

CHAPTER 2

This author prefers to use the phrase "shared decision making" rather than "site-based decision making." This stance is based not only on experience but also on his reading of the recent change literature. Experience would suggest that site-based decision making is the title often given to autonomous decision making at the school site level. Indeed, in the early 1990s, it was often used as the excuse for a school site to virtually secede from the local union.

In a 1996 paper ("Changing the Change Culture: Three Stages of School Improvement"), this author describes how various districts in Iowa have experienced three kinds of leadership style and three concomitant ways of making decisions and going about change. The first style—authoritarian, top-down leadership—led to the formation of a change culture in the school buildings that was characterized by dependency. The next stage—characterized by school-site independence—witnessed the onset of a hands-off leadership style and site-based decision making. The third stage is typified by more interdependence and more collegial and inclusive approaches to decision making and leadership.

In writing this 1996 paper, the author used the following contribution from the curriculum director of a district included in the research:

> During the years, 1985-1990, our district was in a very centralized, "top-down" mode of operation. At that time, our superintendent was a strong, directive, authoritarian administrator who accomplished many things. However, this "take-charge" leader required everyone to conform to district decisions and district directives. Individual building autonomy was not encouraged. All decisions regarding textbook adoptions, for instance, were uniform throughout the district. The budgeting process was firmly in control of the central office.
>
> When that Superintendent left our district, the Assistant Superintendent became Superintendent (1990-1995). Here was a leader with a style in sharp contrast to her predecessor. She was a long-time district employee who had come up through the ranks as teacher, guidance counselor, principal, and assistant superintendent. She was a strong believer in teacher empowerment and site-based decision making. She firmly believed that people closest to the problem were always the best suited to come up with the solution. Under her leadership, trust and staff morale were at an all-time high. Buildings were given significant control over their budgets. Textbook

ELEMENT 6

Continuous Improvement in the Self-Renewing School

adoptions were now a building decision. Buildings were encouraged to come up with pilot programs of initiatives. Schools no longer had to be in lock-step with the rest of the district. Different projects and ways of doing things emerged at the various buildings.

The taste of freedom was heady, and the site-based decision making progressed over the years, until it became teacher-based decision making. Soon, even individual teachers were allowed to select their own curriculum materials—so much so that fourth grade teachers throughout the district might be using nine different reading programs, and several different math books. Even within one school building, different types of books and programs were used. This caused great problems for curriculum and instructional continuity. Many students in our district are transient, and the variety of instructional programs (even at the same grade level) exacerbated disruption when students transferred from one building to another. Parents became aware of the differences between schools and thought that it all seemed very fragmented and disjointed.

Finally, in 1995, we began the third stage of school improvement under the leadership of our current superintendent. Our district school improvement committee is the Transformation Now Team. This is a committee of teachers, administrators, support staff, parents, business, and community representatives. During the 1995-1996 school year, the TNT committee identified four goals:

1. Support school improvement.

2. Create a shared vision for the district.

3. Facilitate communication, both internally and externally.

4. Support school-business partnerships.

In addition, during the 1996-1997 school year, our schools began receiving school improvement leadership training; school improvement teams learned how to develop school improvement plans.

The coordinated efforts of all buildings toward school improvement brought about a sense of continuity and cohesiveness that had previously been lacking. Our approach now is neither "top-down" nor "bottom-up," but rather a combination of both. Good ideas and initiatives flow up and down the system. We have developed a crystal clear focus for our district: school improvement. We are leading systemic change through focused, durable, system-wide improvement in student learning.

ELEMENT 6

Continuous Improvement in the Self-Renewing School

SCHOOL IMPROVEMENT ALIGNMENT

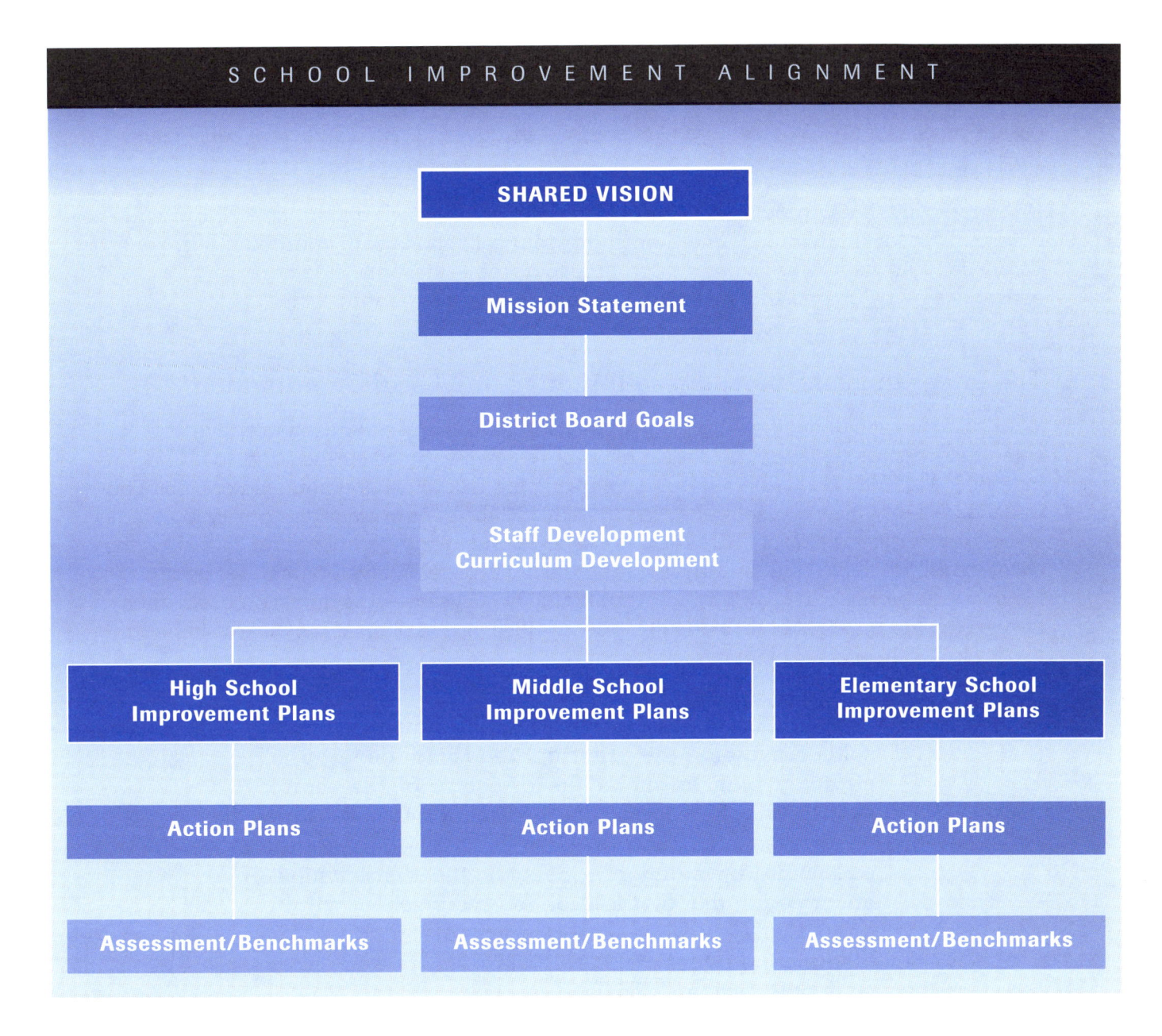

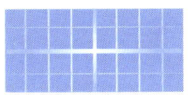

- SHARED VISION
  - Mission Statement
    - District Board Goals
      - Staff Development / Curriculum Development
        - High School Improvement Plans → Action Plans → Assessment/Benchmarks
        - Middle School Improvement Plans → Action Plans → Assessment/Benchmarks
        - Elementary School Improvement Plans → Action Plans → Assessment/Benchmarks

The Self-Renewing School ■ Task 6: Understanding the Difference Between Site-Based and Shared Decision Making

Purpose: To understand the differences between site-based and shared decision making by relating to the case study material.

Grouping: Work individually and then share with your Learning Team.

105

CHAPTER 2

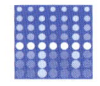

<u>Group process strategy:</u> Meet in a Circle configuration and use a sufficient consensus strategy.

<u>Directions:</u> In what ways does this description mirror your own experiences? How is it different? Reflect individually and then share your reflections with your team — in your Circle configuration. This is also a good time to agree — through "sufficient consensus" — by composing a list of common issues and experiences.

The Integration of School-Based Initiative and Local Coordination

What is significant about the third stage of development is that site-based initiative and commitment is retained and melded within more system-wide coherence and coordination. Indeed, Joyce, Wolf, and Calhoun (1993), following the lead of other commentators, point out that the *district* is the local, self-renewing system and the central office has a very legitimate voice and role to play in shared, system-wide decision making and planning. In fact, as the case described above would suggest, during the third stage of development, the healthy local system probably finds ways of balancing the two (system-wide and site-based), thus harnessing the power of both. Indeed, Feddema (1996) has explained why it is so important to develop both levels of planning in unison:

> Because the district is the strategic unit in a local school system, the district needs to develop a strategic plan to shape the direction of the entire system. District-wide strategic direction is necessary for two reasons. First, the district needs to establish and maintain standards. Second, the district must ensure equitable distribution for every school within a district. It provides the conceptual guidance for creating the future of the entire system, as well as for each of the system's parts.
>
> The district's strategic plan defines the parameters within which school sites must operate and develop their plans. It provides the context that is necessary to ensure responsible decentralization. Without the district plan, people in schools have no frame of reference for determining the appropriateness of their actions. In other words, the district's strategic plan legitimizes plans developed at the local school site.

ELEMENT 6

Continuous Improvement in the Self-Renewing School

Using the district's strategic plan as background information, each school should develop a site-specific plan that complements the district plan. School-site plans promote responsible autonomy by empowering people at the local level to develop and implement plans within the district's framework. It is through the school-site plans that the dreams expressed in the district's strategic plan are transformed into reality for students in their schools.

Developing school-site plans unleashes the creative power and energy of people throughout the system to implement initiatives identified in the strategic plan. The passion for planning tends to be greatest at the school level. Whereas districts are abstractions to most people, schools are "real" organizations which motivate people to extraordinary effort in order to make a difference in the lives of students. Motivation and enthusiasm for achieving excellence are greater when developing school-site rather than strategic plans. When the school-site plans are developed within the context of a district's strategic plan, meaningful improvement is possible throughout the system.

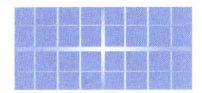

The Self-Renewing School ■ Task 7: Integrating School-Based Initiatives with System Coordination

Purpose: To review the extent to which school-based initiatives and system coordination have been integrated in the participants' school(s).

Grouping: Work with your Learning Team.

Directions: In your Learning Team, respond to the following question:
How have school-based initiatives and system coordination and coherence been integrated in your school district?

CHAPTER 2

Site-based decision making, therefore, can be seen as a sub-set of shared decision making. While site-based decision making has its own importance, it is necessary but not sufficient for making decisions across the entire local system. Everyone agrees, however, that decision making at the local level is the way forward. Barth (1991), in emphasizing that school people are asserting more responsibility for their own schools, maintains that confidence is growing in increased governance and decision making—site-based management he calls it—at the school site. Moreover, he states:

> Many are coming to believe that those closest to students, and those likely to be most affected by the decisions, should make them.

Writing in similar terms, Forsythe (1999) states:

> People who will be held responsible for the results of the decision need to make the decision. Part of the information used to make the decision is input gathered from those who might be affected by the decision but not held accountable for it.

Forsythe makes an interesting distinction here between those responsible for the results of a decision and those impacted by the decision. The former, she says, should make the decision, while the latter should have input to the decision. Indeed, there has been much discussion about who should be legitimately involved in local decision making. During the period when site-based decision making was predominant, it was argued that school staff members should be involved in making all decisions. There are three reasons why this is not feasible.

First, there is the purely practical concern of time management. There just isn't enough time in the day to be involved in all educational decision making—and still teach students. Second, some decisions are somewhat trivial and do not need to be made by a school's faculty collectively. (One person—or a small group of people directly responsible for this service—can decide the lunch menu for the week.) Third, some decisions, regarding, for example, personnel and budget issues, need to be made at the system level—either because of confidentiality issues involved or because those at the system level are more impartial and have the interests of the system in mind and not one section of the system. In other words, says Holly (2003), it is important to have clarity around decision making—*who* will make *which* decisions, *when*, and *how* they will be made.

In terms of the *how*, one possibility has already been introduced: that giving input and making the final decision are different steps within the same decision-making process and may involve different sets of people. Dolan (1994) created a decision-making planning matrix to help educators decide how decisions are going to be made and who is going

ELEMENT 6

Continuous Improvement in the Self-Renewing School

to be involved. One axis of his matrix lists decision-making categories or topics; his examples are curricular and educational, personnel and staffing, financial, and logistical. On the other axis (which he calls the gamut of control and decentralization) he lists those people who will be responsible for making the decisions (Mine; Mine with Explanation; Mine With Input From You, and so forth). Saphier et al. (1989) have some good ideas concerning the categories of involvement to use for this dimension. An outline matrix is included below so that participants can fashion a decision-making planner that works in their situation.

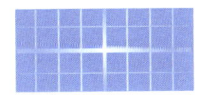

The Self-Renewing School
Task 8: Constructing a Decision-Making Matrix

Purpose: To understand the importance of clarifying who makes which decisions.

Grouping: Work with your Learning Team.

Directions: Using this outline, construct a matrix that would help you and your colleagues to clarify *who* makes *which* decisions in your local situation.

| Decision Topics | Kinds of Involvement |
| (The "What") | (The "Who") |

CHAPTER 2

Making Decisions That Stay Made

Like Dolan, Saphier et al. (1989) have described how to make decisions, especially ones that stay in effect. In order to bind staff members together to make legitimate decisions, they say, the process of decision making has to be improved. Leaders, therefore, have to pay attention to decision-making processes if they expect to enlist faculty support in solving problems, changing instructional practices, and carrying out school improvement plans. Barth (1991) makes much the same point when he says that creating a school improvement plan doesn't make for school improvement; it is, he says, collegiality and collaborative decision making that make all the difference. Indeed, Saphier et al. identify twelve guidelines for making good decisions:

1. Identify the issue or goal.

2. Find out how much discretion there is in taking action in this area.

3. Determine who will make the preliminary and final decision:

    - an individual or group above you in the organization
    - you as administrator unilaterally
    - you as administrator with input from staff
    - you as administrator and staff by consensus
    - staff with input from you as administrator
    - staff by consensus
    - staff by vote
    - subgroup of staff, with input from others
    - subgroup of staff unilaterally
    - individual staff members unilaterally

4. Communicate who will make the decision.

5. State the non-negotiable issues.

6. Determine the full consequences of the decision.

7. Involve all parties whose working conditions will be affected by the decision.

8. Make clear the timeline for deciding and implementing the decision.

9. Decide. Issue a statement containing the key points of the decision.

ELEMENT 6

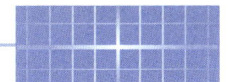

Continuous Improvement in the Self-Renewing School

10. Provide for review, evaluation, and revision of the decision.

11. Close the loop—communicate the reasons for the decision to all affected parties.

12. Plan how to monitor and support the implementation of the decision.

The Self-Renewing School ■ Task 9: Reviewing the Guidelines for Making Good Decisions

<u>Purpose:</u> To identify what is still not clear about local decision-making arrangements.

<u>Grouping:</u> Work with your Learning Team.

<u>Directions:</u> Looking at this list of twelve points as a team, which are still in need of clarification in your local situation?

CHAPTER 2

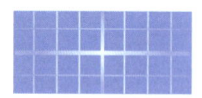

The Self-Renewing School
Task 10: Composing a Common Public Agreement

Purpose: To compose (or revise, if one exists) a "Common Public Agreement" for local decision making.

Grouping: Work with your Learning Team.

Directions: Given the frustrations that occur when some of these points are left unclear, Calhoun (1994) has endorsed the writing of common public agreements concerning how decisions are to be made. Much of the clarity needed to guide shared decision making, she says, should be encapsulated in a constitution or charter that describes how school-wide decisions are made and specifies the areas in which teachers and administrators will be equally responsible for decisions.

Please insert here *either* an existing decision-making charter or one that you and your colleagues write as a result of reading this section.

ELEMENT 6

Continuous Improvement in the Self-Renewing School

Voting in Decision Making

Hatch (2002) has questioned the validity of voting in decision making.

> Almost all exploration processes end with a vote in which the teachers, school staff members, or members of the larger school community are given a chance to decide whether to move ahead with the implementation of a program.
>
> These "buy-in" votes are often little more than perfunctory exercises that can easily be manipulated by principals and other powerful members of the school community. Votes may demonstrate not that the school has built the capacity to make an informed choice but that the ad campaign for the program has been effective.

The Self-Renewing School ■ Task 11: Understanding the Impact of Voting in the Decision-Making Process

<u>Purpose:</u> To understand the shortcomings of "voting" as a decision-making procedure.

<u>Grouping:</u> Work individually.

<u>Directions:</u> In your experience, are these criticisms justified? Give examples. If so, how can they be avoided? Record your thoughts below.

CHAPTER 2

The Downside of Shared Decision Making

Indeed, because of the institutional inertia—the "dynamic conservatism" described by Donald Schon (1971)—built into larger educational organizations, staff votes—like other methods—could merely give the participants new and collective powers of veto, thus determining that no new, significant changes could get through their safety net. This could be called the self-vetoing prophecy as opposed to the self-fulfilling prophecy. It could be said that there has been more energy devoted to winning educators' rights to be involved in decision making than how they should respond when given the opportunity. With rights, it is true, come responsibilities.

Those educators who fight to be involved in decision making only to use their new-found powers to block any substantial investment in change initiatives should be reminded that decision making is not an end in itself (or another bone to fight over in the power struggle of "them-versus-us"); it is for the judicious application of school improvement and the enhancement of student learning. Decision making is the means not the end. The acid test, of course, is whether shared decision making is used as a dam or a sluice gate. The former approach involves a blanket rejection of change; the latter entails the prudent application of a filtering system that rejects unnecessary changes, but that opens in response to changes that are identified as necessary to the continuing growth of the self-regulating organism.

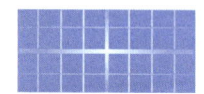

The Self-Renewing School
Task 12: Filtering Change

Purpose: To understand the importance of building safeguards that protect participants against the downside of shared decision making.

LT

Grouping: Work with your Learning Team.

Directions: In your Learning Team, discuss what safeguards can be used to ameliorate the downside of shared decision making.

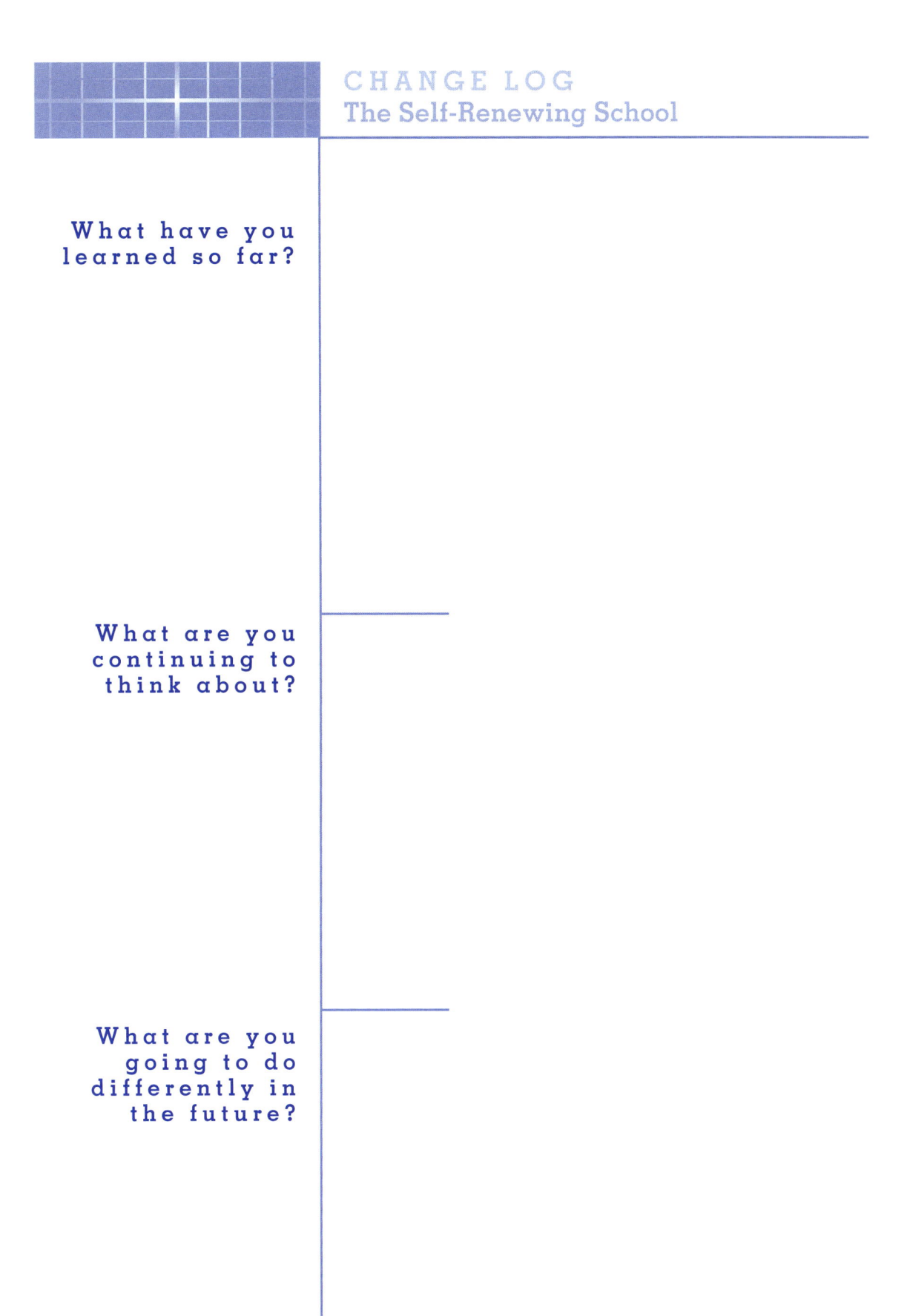

CHANGE LOG
The Self-Renewing School

What have you learned so far?

What are you continuing to think about?

What are you going to do differently in the future?

Notes

Element 7

Creating a Data-Driven School Culture

Overview

The goal is to establish a data-driven school culture. Experience tells us that several factors are crucial in the establishment of such a culture: the embedding of data literacy throughout the local system (involving the deployment of trained data coaches—or their equivalent—and the construction of data profiles at all four system levels), the organization of a team-based infrastructure for local data-based decision making, and the kind of supportive, collaborative leadership style that is consonant with participatory management.

It is vital to establish an infrastructure that is not only well organized and inter-connected but also involves the utilization of effective team-processing skills—of the kind used throughout this workbook. The aim is to be inclusive and capitalize on the contributions of a wide range of participants—thus generating their continuing commitment as the heart and soul of the enterprise. Major skills utilized here are necessarily organizational ones. Data coaches, for instance, have to be skilled in data use and in establishing good rapport with other staff members; they have to connect with both data and colleagues. More generally, good communication skills and collaborative leadership skills are certainly required, as are team-building and team-processing skills. Indeed, it is the quality of the teamwork that makes or breaks this whole initiative.

The healthy self-renewing local system uses both shared decision making and data-based deliberation as triggers for continuous school improvement. Such a system can be said to have a data-driven culture, the ingredients of which have been identified by Noyce, Perda, and Traver (2000). Holly (2000) adapted these same elements in composing a survey to which educators can respond by indicating the degree to which such a culture has become embedded in their particular situation (refer to Task 1 that follows).

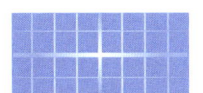

Creating a Data-Driven School Culture
Task 1: Identifying Strengths and Challenges

Purpose: Participants are to use the following questionnaire to identify the strengths and challenges in their development of a data-driven school culture.

Grouping: Work individually and then meet with your Learning Team.

Group process strategy: Use a Consensus Building strategy.

CHAPTER 2

<u>Directions:</u> This is another major task for you and your colleagues. You are asked to follow these instructions:

1. Fill in the questionnaire that follows individually.

2. Collate your individual responses and agree upon a "consensus version" for your group.

3. Identify the strengths and challenges of your local system and list them below.

Strengths   **Challenges**

ELEMENT 7
Creating a Data-Driven School Culture

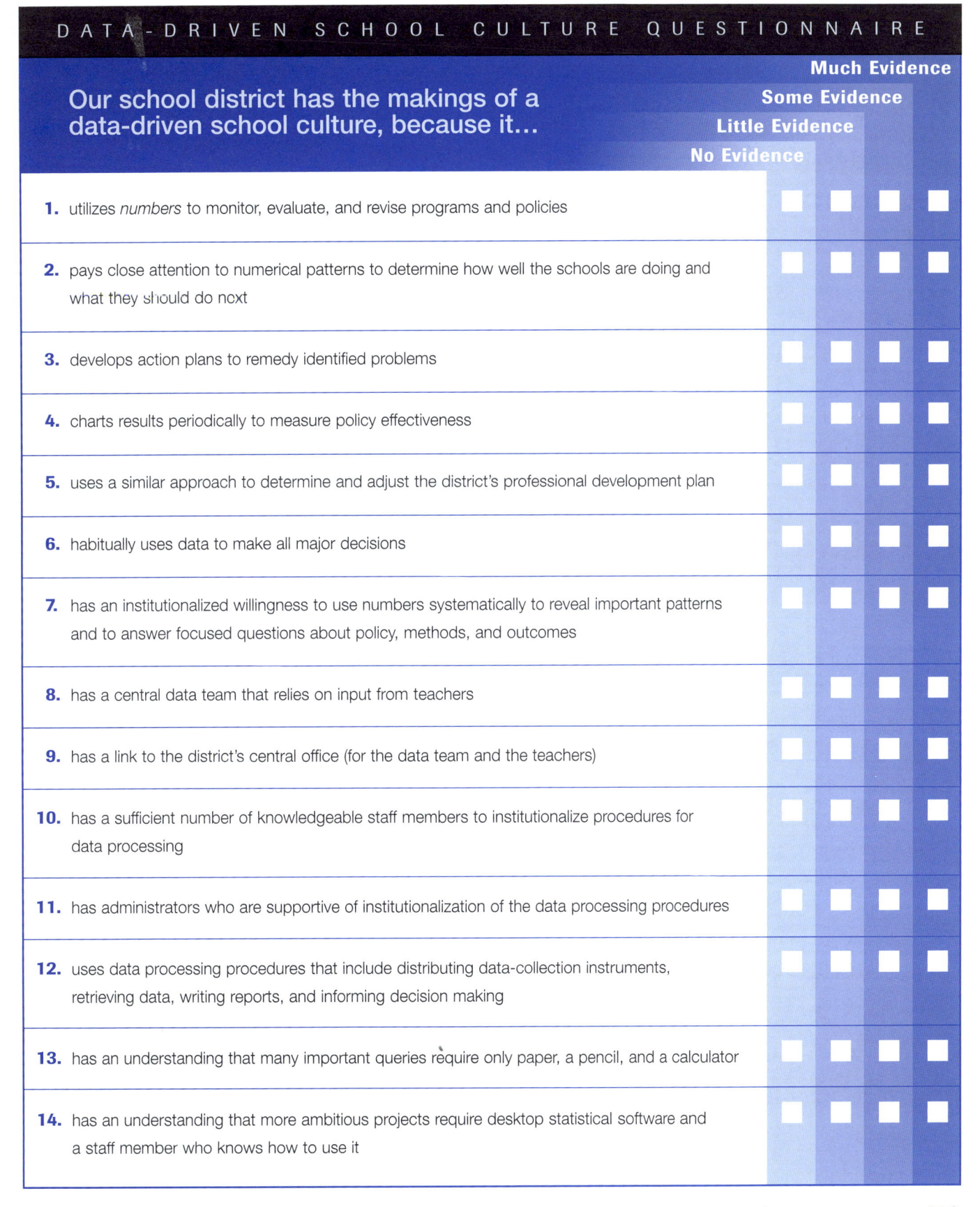

DATA-DRIVEN SCHOOL CULTURE QUESTIONNAIRE

Our school district has the makings of a data-driven school culture, because it…

	Much Evidence	Some Evidence	Little Evidence	No Evidence

1. utilizes *numbers* to monitor, evaluate, and revise programs and policies ☐ ☐ ☐ ☐

2. pays close attention to numerical patterns to determine how well the schools are doing and what they should do next ☐ ☐ ☐ ☐

3. develops action plans to remedy identified problems ☐ ☐ ☐ ☐

4. charts results periodically to measure policy effectiveness ☐ ☐ ☐ ☐

5. uses a similar approach to determine and adjust the district's professional development plan ☐ ☐ ☐ ☐

6. habitually uses data to make all major decisions ☐ ☐ ☐ ☐

7. has an institutionalized willingness to use numbers systematically to reveal important patterns and to answer focused questions about policy, methods, and outcomes ☐ ☐ ☐ ☐

8. has a central data team that relies on input from teachers ☐ ☐ ☐ ☐

9. has a link to the district's central office (for the data team and the teachers) ☐ ☐ ☐ ☐

10. has a sufficient number of knowledgeable staff members to institutionalize procedures for data processing ☐ ☐ ☐ ☐

11. has administrators who are supportive of institutionalization of the data processing procedures ☐ ☐ ☐ ☐

12. uses data processing procedures that include distributing data-collection instruments, retrieving data, writing reports, and informing decision making ☐ ☐ ☐ ☐

13. has an understanding that many important queries require only paper, a pencil, and a calculator ☐ ☐ ☐ ☐

14. has an understanding that more ambitious projects require desktop statistical software and a staff member who knows how to use it ☐ ☐ ☐ ☐

continued on next page

CHAPTER 2

DATA-DRIVEN SCHOOL CULTURE QUESTIONNAIRE

Our school district has the makings of a data-driven school culture, because it...

#	Statement	No Evidence	Little Evidence	Some Evidence	Much Evidence
15.	makes a determined effort to use data to become more informed and confident about the progress and impact of program policy and methods	☐	☐	☐	☐
16.	has a common acceptance that data knowledge allows for proactive demands for accountability	☐	☐	☐	☐
17.	has a major motivating individual who promotes and supports acceptance of a data-driven culture	☐	☐	☐	☐
18.	provides technical and financial supports for data collection, analysis, and communication	☐	☐	☐	☐
19.	has consultants to augment these efforts	☐	☐	☐	☐
20.	has teachers who are viewed as essential members of all the activities and who are prepared to both provide data and then use it to improve their classroom practice	☐	☐	☐	☐
21.	has data teams that are willing to enhance or develop computerized information management systems within their district	☐	☐	☐	☐
22.	has data teams that are willing to collect and analyze data related to specific research questions	☐	☐	☐	☐

Establishing a Data-Based Culture

The author (2000) has also listed what it takes to establish a data-based culture:

- understanding that continuous improvement is needs-based and data-driven
- committing to data-based and, therefore, informed decision making at all levels of the local system
- generating a capacity for data use throughout the system
- ensuring that all those in the system acquire data literacy
- establishing data use as part of our way of life

ELEMENT 7

Creating a Data-Driven School Culture

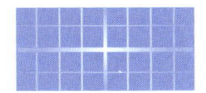

Creating a Data-Driven School Culture
Task 2: Summarizing Survey Findings

Purpose: To summarize findings from the previous activity.

Grouping: Work with your Learning Team.

Directions: Review your "consensus version" of responses to the survey in Task 1 as well as the points raised. Where is your school district in the establishment of a data-based school culture? Please ring one of the statements below — the one that *best* describes your situation.

- We are non-starters.

- We know what has to be done and have begun to move forward.

- We're getting there.

- We're well advanced.

- We're firing on all cylinders.

Explain your response in detail. Provide examples.

One District with a Data-Based Culture

In Dubuque Schools in Dubuque, Iowa, a concerted effort has been made over several years to create such a data-based school (and district) culture. Two moves in particular have added real impetus to this initiative: the construction of Data Profiles and the

121

assignment of Data Coaches. Data Profiles are being established at four system levels: the student, the classroom teacher, the school, and the district. Each profile is a database (an electronic version of the student profile is currently being prepared), a kind of data-bank account into which deposits—and from which withdrawals—can be made. It is envisaged that such "transactions" will be ongoing and that the profile will be constantly in use. Once created and, thereafter, continuously updated, the profiles can be used at all four system levels for very similar purposes (Holly, 2003). Each profile can be used to

- gain new insights and new learnings
- make so-called "in-flight" adjustments
- report to various audiences, both informally and formally
- check on progress toward the shared, long-term vision
- provide feedback
- identify changing data patterns and changing needs
- re-work existing goals and/or set new goals
- amend action plans
- monitor progress and goal achievement
- store baseline data, up-close data, and trend-line data
- show growth over time
- provide the material for accountability

As an important by-product of working on four kinds of Data Profiles, staff members in Dubuque have come to understand the importance of using the same data for four different purposes: district improvement, school improvement, classroom teacher improvement, and the improvement of student learning. They also understand much more about the importance of aggregating and disaggregating the same data and allowing data to flow in both directions across the system. District data can now be disaggregated for each school; school data disaggregated for each classroom; and classroom data disaggregated for each student. Similarly, individual student data can be collated and aggregated for use at the classroom level; classroom data can be aggregated for school use; and school data aggregated for district use. Moreover, when the members of a school faculty complete their item analysis of, for example, the Iowa Test of Basic Skills (ITBS), they can ask questions that embrace all four system levels:

ELEMENT 7

Creating a Data-Driven School Culture

- What is our contribution to the achievements of the district?

- How are we doing as a building? What are our strengths and challenges?

- How am I doing in my classroom? What are my strengths and challenges?

- How is each student doing? What are his or her strengths and challenges?

Conzemius (2000) has argued that an education system must develop a proper context for data-driven school improvement. The challenge, she says, is to create a culture for accountability based on professional standards of mutual respect, collegial learning, and **regular, open, honest conversations about student performance**. Such a culture is well on the road to fruition in Dubuque Schools.

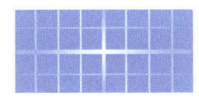

Creating a Data-Driven School Culture ■ Task 3: Reflecting on Local Efforts in Light of Dubuque Schools' Efforts

Purpose: To review local efforts in the light of case study material.

LT

Grouping: Work with your Learning Team.

Directions: Reflecting as a team upon what is being done with data across Dubuque Schools, what could your own school system gain from Dubuque's experience? Do there appear to be any drawbacks? Why?

The Pivotal Role Of Data Coach

Another boost for data-based decision making in Dubuque Schools has come from the local training program for "Data Coaches" representing each building. This program is now entering its third year. The training sessions involve small teams from each building (the principal and at least two staff members) who are expected to replicate their learning experiences with colleagues back at school. The idea of creating Data Coaches was first suggested by Tom Bellamy as part of his attempts to implement "The Cycles of School Improvement" (see Bellamy, Holly, and Sinisi, 1997). His conclusion was that, for data-driven school improvement efforts to really succeed, capacity for data use had to be increased at the local level.

CHAPTER 2

As the title "Data Coach" suggests, it is a two-sided concept. First, it involves having a facility with the kind of data that are used every day in education—both quantitative and qualitative data included. Second, it involves being a mentor for others to be able to enter the "data club." As the leading data coach for the building, the principal has to exhibit the same level of skill in data use and the ability to support other colleagues in acquiring the same skill set. Working together, the Data Coaches have two home-based tasks: one is to increase the level of skill and knowledge across the staff and the other is to turn this capacity-building exercise into a culture-building initiative. Data use has to become the "way we do things around here." According to Noyce, Perda, and Traver (2000):

> When districts and schools use data to make decisions, they have the makings of a data-driven school culture...Data-driven school cultures do not arise in a vacuum. They need a major motivator and technical and financial support.

Recently, Holly and Lange (2001) presented a report to the Dubuque administration under the title, "Establishing a Culture of Data-Based School Improvement." The most "advanced sites" (those with the most experience in using data to inform school-improvement decisions), the report states, are realizing the following:

- Data collection is not a one time only activity; it is a continuous and ongoing concern.

- In a five-year planning/implementation sequence (as expected of all school districts in Iowa), any changes in the plan should reflect any changes in the data.

- Data collection, therefore, is not going away; it's not a temporary fad. It's becoming an organic part of our way of life in schools and districts.

- Some of the data collected on an ongoing basis speaks directly to the progress being made on school goals; other data not directly related to current goals may well flag the existence of new, emerging areas of need. Student learning needs are ever changing and so is the data that speaks to these needs. We have to be fleet-of-foot in responding to these new data-based needs. Student mobility and transiency, for instance, has become a major issue in Dubuque Schools—in a matter of months.

- The best way to stay on top of this need to collect data that both speak to existing goals and signal new, emerging goals is to build a School Data Profile that is constantly in use.

- Within a comparatively short space of time, the Data Coaches have entered the life-blood of Dubuque Schools.

ELEMENT 7

Creating a Data-Driven School Culture

Gathering Around the Data

Holly and Lange (2002) have also listed the techniques that the Data Coaches have used to establish themselves and their work at the site level:

- They have encouraged the use of a school improvement/data collection calendar.

- They have encouraged the ongoing collection of up-close data which, according to one staff, allowed them to "gather around the data."

- They have played a central role in directing and coordinating a school's improvement efforts—by being linked to the Site Council on one side and the staff generally on the other. Interestingly, by having what amounts to a roving brief and not being identified with one particular committee (they are normally "co-opted," ex-officio members of the Site Council), the most effective Data Coaches have been able to permeate the membranes of their schools.

- They have encouraged more recording, reviewing of progress, and reporting on the part of school-based action teams—and, therefore, more process (and product) accountability.

- They have advocated for the selection of goals and priorities that are needs-based and data-driven and not interest-based (and seen as "good ideas at the time"). The message has been that there are many excellent strategies out there, but which ones really suit our needs?

- They have combined the ideas from Data Coach Training with the need to produce other reports or profiles. For instance, high schools involved in the North Central Association (NCA) school accreditation process are expected to build the work around a School Profile—so the suggested framework was introduced for all sites in Dubuque to follow—as a guide for their efforts.

- They need to keep doing everything that can be done to transfer ownership of the data-driven school improvement process to the classroom level. Without this, the whole initiative will be seriously impaired.

Holly and Lange (2002) have used this seven-point agenda as a self-assessment tool for Data Coaches (see the following page).

Typical responses from participants in the Data Coach training sessions have included such comments as:

- "We now have the ability to compare, show growth, identify strengths and weaknesses."

- "Previously, we haven't been used to sharing our data—for the good of students—it's no longer for my eyes only."

CHAPTER 2

- "We can now use a spreadsheet of interventions—did this child have preschool, Title 1, Reading Recovery, summer school, and so forth."

- "Our changes are now data-based and not merely interest-based; we can ask 'why are we using this strategy?'—and find out that it's not necessarily according to data."

SELF-ASSESSMENT OF CURRENT ROLES OF DATA COACHES

Role	Importance Rating 1-5 (5=very important)	Current Status (1-5)	Needs (to be included in Action Plan)
Encourage the use of a school improvement/data collection calendar.			
Encourage the ongoing collection of up-close data — "gathering around the data."			
Play a central role in directing/coordinating a school's improvement efforts — by being linked to the site council and the staff in general.			
Encourage more recording/progress reviewing/reporting on the part of action team members — and therefore, more process accountability.			
Advocate for the selection of goals/priorities that are needs based and data driven and not interest based or just an excellent strategy.			
Combine the ideas from data coach training with the need to produce other reports or profiles, e.g., NCA or Title I.			
Do everything that can be done to transfer ownership of the process to the classroom level.			

(Holly and Lange, 2002)

ELEMENT 7

Creating a Data-Driven School Culture

Creating a Data-Driven School Culture
Task 4: Reflecting on Data Coach Training

Purpose: To reflect on the potential of Data Coach Training for strengthening a data-driven Culture.

Grouping: Work with your Learning Team.

Directions: How might Data Coach Training enhance your efforts to establish a data-driven school culture? Please discuss as a team.

Using Data Effectively

Conzemius (2000) has good advice to offer those in any district trying to establish a data-driven school culture. She says, for example:

> Good data-driven decision making extends well beyond simply testing students for achievement and reporting discrete numbers and grades as indicators of success. Data-driven school improvement encompasses myriad qualitative and quantitative measures, which are gathered and analyzed within a culture that embraces, respects, celebrates, and expects continuous improvement and learning for adults and children alike.

CHAPTER 2

The effective use of data, she says, depends on four basic elements: focus; reflection; collaboration; and transformational leadership.

Focus, according to Conzemius, is about creating clarity of thought, direction, and purpose. As the author has argued in this workbook, Conzemius underscores:

> Data-driven school improvement starts with identifying organizational purpose, vision, and values. Educators then align their improvement efforts with standards and measurable, targeted goals.

At that point, of course, data genuinely become our best friends. They help us know the measure of our success.

Reflection is what we do with data; we think about what they are telling us. Reflection, as an iterative process, lies at the heart of data-driven school improvement. Thought and action are reciprocal partners in the improvement process.

According to the same author:

> Reflection means providing feedback to the system — both hard numbers and qualitative assessments — about how well it is accomplishing its goals. As we contemplate the meaning of assessment results and seriously research the efficacy of our actions, we heighten our ability to make informed and reasoned decisions about our practice. This is what distinguishes the professional practitioner from the technician.

ELEMENT 7
Creating a Data-Driven School Culture

> Reflection answers the questions, "Where are we now?" and "What are we learning?" Reflection gives us a means for going beyond our best guess or informed hunch about what is working or not working. Reflection provides a comprehensive view of the dynamics of learning within and throughout the system. By taking time to reflect on what we are learning about our practice, we can actually speed up the improvement process. In systems as complex as schools, slowing down to think, learn, and plan will lead to better long-term outcomes.

Slowing down to go faster is an interesting concept. Similar to the battle-cry "less is more" (and, indeed, connected to it), it sounds counter-intuitive. In the experience of such districts as Dubuque, it is certainly not counter-productive. When a school takes time out to "sharpen the saw" (Covey, 1989), collect relevant data, really study the messages contained therein, and then plan accordingly, future school improvement efforts seem more effortless—and definitely more focused and swifter in their application. It all seems to come together.

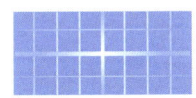

A Data-Driven School Culture
Task 5: Finding Time to Learn From Data

<u>Purpose:</u> To learn by doing—to understand the importance of finding the time to learn from data by writing a script that can be used to argue the case with colleagues.

<u>Grouping:</u> Work individually and then meet with your Learning Team.

<u>Directions:</u> If one of your colleagues were to say to you, "We haven't got time to collect data," how might you respond? Reflect on this question individually and then write a "script" as a team, where you respond to this colleague.

CHAPTER 2

Conzemius also reminds us:

> It's important not to confuse reflection with inspection. Reflection exists within a culture whose core value is learning and improvement. Inspection, on the other hand, exists within a culture whose core value is blame. Inspection is a defects-driven notion, while reflection is a growth-driven process. In a positive organizational culture, reflection is a nurturing process that helps guide important decision making.

This is a crucial point. Data-driven, reflective school improvement processes will soon whither in an antipathetic environment and climate where "Gotcha!" is the way of life. Likewise, it will flourish in the kind of culture that Barth (2002) has recently described as one that "creates and sustains a community of student and adult learning" and where the faculty members are invited to become "observers of the old and architects of the new." Barth emphasizes that every school has a culture; some are hospitable, he says, and others are toxic. Above all, a school's culture can work for or against improvement and reform.

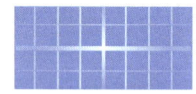

Creating a Data-Driven School Culture
Task 6: Reflecting on Your School Culture

Purpose: To reflect on whether local schools/districts have the kind of cultures that would support open, honest data-based dialogue.

Grouping: Work with your Learning Team.

Directions: Reflect as a team on the following crucial question:

Does your school and/or school district have the kind of culture that would support reflective, honest, and open dialogue? Why or why not and give examples.

ELEMENT 7

Creating a Data-Driven School Culture

Collaborative Leadership

Two factors that Barth (2002) says can contribute to changing a school culture are the third and fourth elements recommended by Conzemius. They are **collaboration** and **leadership**. Without a collaborative approach, she says:

> Focus and reflection can easily lead us down our own narrow and biased path to conclusions that support what we think we already know. The greatest value of collaboration is the diversity of thought and perspective that it brings to creative endeavors.

Moreover, stresses Conzemius, it is the use of data that keeps teamwork focused, substantive, and productive. As for leadership, she says, the top priority of the transformational leader is to create a safe place for learning and improvement. Many commentators would agree. Barth (2002), Holly (2003), Hessel and Holloway (2002), Forsythe (1996) and Calhoun (1999) among many have underlined the need for skilled and supportive leadership in the formation of a learning community. Indeed, the collective message is that leadership—like culture—can make or break the endeavor. For her part, Calhoun (1999) concludes:

> In my 28 years of experience, there is nothing as critical to school implementation of new teaching strategies as the principal's full participation in learning the strategy, practicing in the classroom, sharing with his or her peer coaching group how students responded, and building the next lessons together. I can almost map a school's level of implementation by how engaged the principal is in modeling what is happening.

CHAPTER 2

Forsythe (1996) has argued that, in the new collaborative workplace, leadership is more important not less. Talking about the role of principal as school leader, she says:

> The emphasis on the initiative of teachers in successful school improvement does not in any way diminish or supplant the role of the principal in that process. In fact, the importance of the principal is increased, not decreased, by the engagement of teachers in the school improvement process.

The author (2003) has identified four leadership styles based on a simple frame. By using two axes (informal to formal and hands-on to hands-off) and inter-connecting them, four leadership styles emerge—see below. One style is Informal-Hands-On; a second is Formal-Hands-On; a third is Formal-Hands-Off; and a fourth is Informal-Hands-Off.

Leadership Style

	Hands-On	
Informal-Hands-On		Formal-Hands-On
Informal		**Formal**
Informal-Hands-Off		Formal-Hands-Off
	Hands-Off	

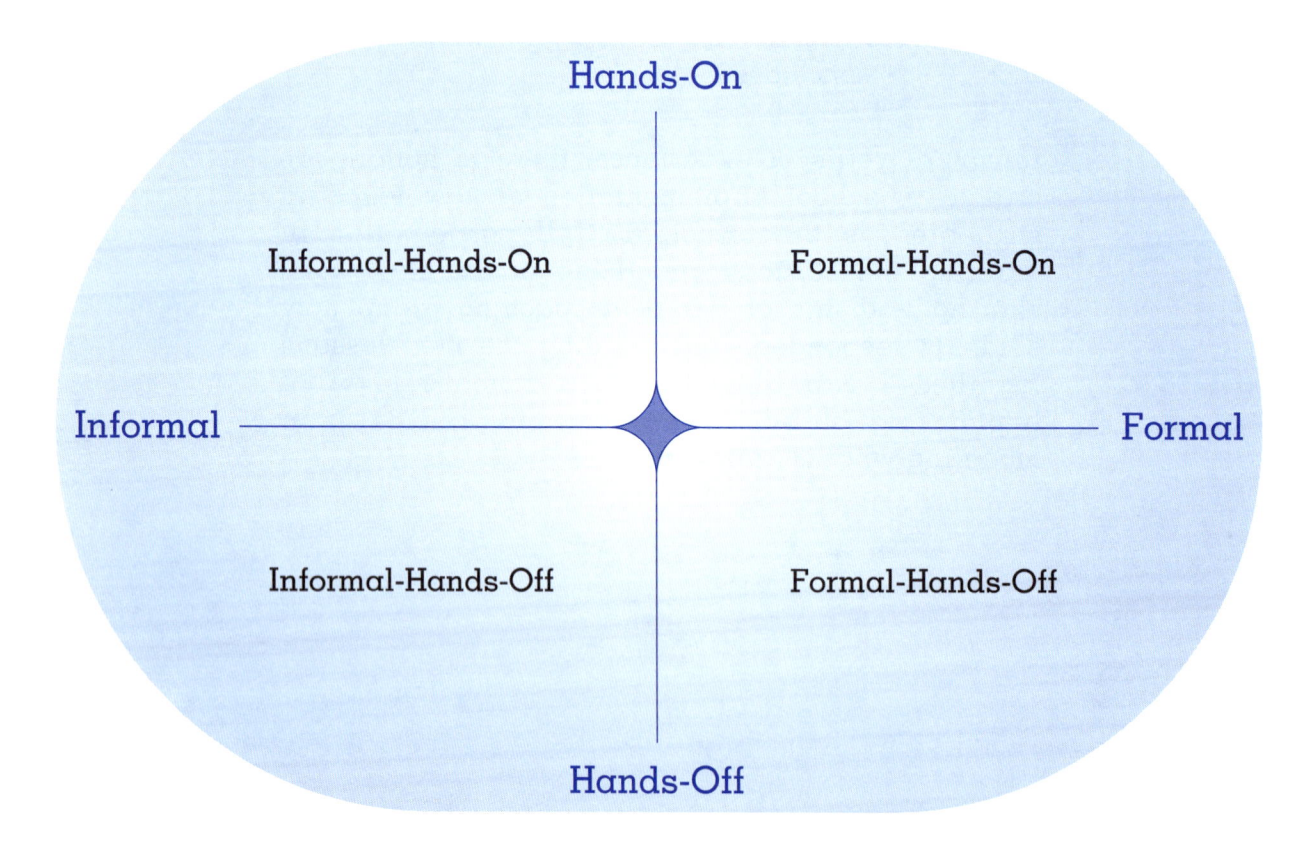

ELEMENT 7

Creating a Data-Driven School Culture

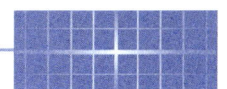

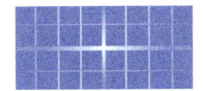

Creating a Data-Driven School Culture
Task 7: Identifying an Effective Leadership Style

Purpose: To identify the leadership style that is most conducive for continuous school improvement efforts.

Grouping: Work with your Learning Team.

Directions: As a team, first discuss the advantages and disadvantages of each style for change leadership, and then decide which of these four styles would be most conducive for leading continuous school improvement efforts. Justify your selection by developing a list of reasons why your team thinks that you have chosen the best of the four styles.

Best style for leadership of school improvement:

List of reasons:

CHAPTER 2

Establishing an Infrastructure for Continuous School Improvement

Another crucial factor in determining success is the establishment of an **infrastructure** for school improvement. Experience in Dubuque Schools would suggest that the effective processing of school improvement efforts is much more reliant on the establishment of an interconnected network of teams and committees than is sometimes acknowledged in the research literature. Process and structure are mutually dependent, as are teamwork and a team structure. Moreover, in Dubuque Schools, it has taken ten years to put everything in place—and the job probably isn't finished yet. This infrastructure is what Gardner refers to as "…a system or framework within which continuous innovations, renewal and rebirth can occur."

The infrastructure for continuous school improvement has to be an enabling framework, a system that involves various interconnected teams in key activities such as decision making, data processing, planning, and monitoring progress over time.

In Dubuque, at the school level, the Site Council has a central importance. Composed of representatives of parents, business partners, faculty, staff, and administration, it is the Site Council that directs the work of school improvement in each building. Generally, this works well now—but only because, in the early 1990s, participants were trained by consultant Jim Mitchell in how to create effective leadership teams. His advice was well received. He argued:

- Site Councils must stay focused on student achievement.

- All constituencies need to be represented and have an equal voice at the Site Council (teachers, support staff, administrators, parents, students, business partners/community).

- Each Site Council member represents a constituency and needs to be in communication with those represented.

- The members of each Site Council need to know what their essential work is and articulate that to staff and parents.

- Successful Site Councils keep students out in front, not staff issues.

- Successful Site Councils keep looking for ways to improve.

- The main work of the Site Council is to develop, implement, and assist the School Improvement Plan. This involves:

    - gathering input for development of the School Improvement Plan

    - reviewing and examining school data

ELEMENT 7
Creating a Data-Driven School Culture

- writing the School Improvement Plan (or designating a group to write it based on the Council's established priorities)

- creating Action Teams to accomplish the goals of the School Improvement Plan

- ensuring that the Action Teams know their responsibilities and report progress to the Site Council, the members of which support, encourage, give feedback on the action plans and on the work of the Action Teams, and work with collected assessment data

A committee is currently working in Dubuque to complete the template for an electronic student information management system—to be used across the district. It is interesting to note, therefore, that Jim Mitchell, in his training materials used in Dubuque in the early 1990s, argued:

> Schools should use data collection and analysis to decide priorities and measure progress toward goals....Successful schools have and use a database of information about the school and its students to guide the future direction and to measure progress toward goals.

Indeed, the effective operation of Site Councils in Dubuque, ten years on, is testament to the thoroughness of the original training sessions. Such details as team member roles (facilitator, chairperson, recorder, and evaluator) were covered, as were the basic responsibilities of Site Councils.

- Select the representative membership.

- Assign roles.

- Develop operational norms.

- Define and communicate the essential work.

- Develop the School Improvement Plan.

- Support and coordinate work of the Action Teams.

- Receive data collection and analysis from the Action Teams.

CHAPTER 2

Since the original training for Site Council members, the role of Data Coach has been inserted to augment the school-based improvement efforts. While this role is more flexible, it is a crucial element within the infrastructure for school improvement. Data Coaches service the data needs of both the Site Council and the Action Teams while taking care not to usurp the roles and responsibilities of the members of either. Indeed, part of the success in Dubuque can be attributed to the fact that roles and responsibilities are taken very seriously. The expectation, for instance, is that action teams in each building will regularly issue a progress report to their respective Site Council—and paperwork is provided for this task. Indeed, in the Appendix of this workbook, you will find the paperwork that is currently used in Dubuque Schools to guide the work of both Site Councils and Action Teams.

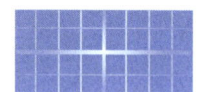

Creating a Data-Driven School Culture
Task 8: Rating the Effectiveness of the Site Council

Purpose: To rate the effectiveness of the Site Council (or its equivalent) in each of the participants' schools.

Grouping: Work individually.

Directions: Using a "1–5" scale (1 being "low" and 5 being "high"), rate each of the following features of your Site Council—or its equivalent—in terms of the degree of application:

Site Council Evaluation

____ Purpose

____ Representation

____ Roles and responsibilities

____ Operational norms

____ Two-way communication

____ Involvement in school improvement planning

____ Coordination of Action Teams

ELEMENT 7
Creating a Data-Driven School Culture

The Next Challenge

When, in 2001, the leaders of the Dubuque school improvement efforts reviewed their ten years of endeavor, they produced this list of key understandings.

- Student learning is the focus: it is essential to "keep our eye on the prize."

- School improvement is continuous, involving annual revisions of the previous plan.

- These revisions should be needs-based and data-driven (and not just a good idea at the time).

- The annual process needs to be as streamlined, integrated, and user-friendly as possible.

- The process and paperwork used has to be as predictable as possible.

- District, school, classroom, and individual student improvement efforts have to be aligned, connected, and mutually supportive.

- A school's capacity for ongoing data use is enhanced by the deployment of trained data coaches.

- Implementation is key; planning is necessary but not sufficient.

- Improved student learning results are expectation #1.

Improvement efforts in Dubuque are ongoing. Current work includes the development of the student information management system and the four kinds of Data Profile. The overall goal, however, is to complete the transfer of the momentum for school improvement to the classroom level, always remembering that what is needed are: self-regulating, data-driven, reflective schools and classrooms where data are the currency of meeting kids' needs (Holly, 1999).

CHAPTER 2

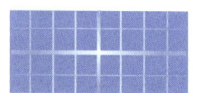

Creating a Data-Driven School Culture
Task 9: Developing an Action Plan

Purpose: To build an action plan that addresses all the challenges identified in this element.

Grouping: Work with your Learning Team.

Directions: As a team, review all the task assignments you have undertaken in this workbook, compile and prioritize a definitive list of the challenges that are facing your school and school district, and then work on an action plan to tackle these challenges.

ELEMENT 7

Creating a Data-Driven School Culture

The Heart and Soul of School Improvement

Data-driven school improvement efforts, to be effective, need supportive processes and structures. Those involved also need to commit to the enterprise **heart and soul**. As Peter Block (1993) has reminded us:

> In any reform effort, the hardest change is the inside work, the emotional work. Creating partnership in a work setting is a shift in beliefs and a personal shift in the way we make contact with those in power. And with those we have power over. These are issues for the artist in us to revisit. Our first instinct is to want to engineer change. To focus on what is outside of us. It is easiest to change those things that are easiest to talk about. So we focus on structure, roles, responsibilities. We have intense discussions about innovative pay systems, self-management strategies, and the elements of total quality management. Discussion of what is concrete and visible and measurable is the engineer in us at work. The engineering work of reform is the actual redesign effort. It is essential, but it is not enough. Something more is required. There is artwork to be done, internal seeing and reevaluation of our own wants, longings, and expectations. If there is no transformation inside each of us, all the structural change in the world will have no impact on our institutions. The moment we think we get the point, and others don't, it is back to square one.

It is the same with data-driven school improvement. Processes and enabling structures are necessary but not sufficient. Participants need opportunities to develop emotional attachment to what is being asked of them. Recent research has highlighted the importance of matching so-called "above-the-line activities" (the technical and behavioral side of change) with "below-the-line activities" (the generation of common values, beliefs, and attitudes—the soul of organizational unity). As Peter Block emphasizes, the one doesn't happen without the other.

CHAPTER 2

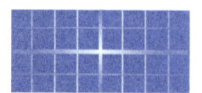

Creating a Data-Driven School Culture
Task 10: Sharing New Ideas with Colleagues

Purpose: To determine how to extend the ideas contained in the workbook to colleagues not involved in the training sessions—in ways that will mobilize their involvement and commitment.

Grouping: Work with your Learning Team.

Directions: With your Learning Team, discuss and plan how to take the ideas of this workbook to your colleagues in ways that will generate their emotional and intellectual attachment and commitment.

In Conclusion

This workbook has presented a new way of going about change in education. In the experience of the consultant-author, it is one that works—for schools and school districts. To use David Tyack's apt description, it is a change process that neither threatens those schools that already work (Tyack, 1999) nor lets those schools off the hook that have been reluctant to rise to the challenge of change. Using data-based decision making as the foundation of the change process creates a soundness, a groundedness, that has previously eluded us.

In a recent report entitled, "Using Data to Improve Schools: What's Working" (AASA, 2002), it is argued that the approach outlined in this workbook fulfills several purposes. Data can be used to

- measure student progress
- make sure students don't fall through the cracks
- measure program effectiveness
- assess instructional effectiveness
- guide curriculum development
- allocate resources wisely
- promote accountability
- report to the community

ELEMENT 7

Creating a Data-Driven School Culture

- meet state and federal reporting requirements
- maintain educational focus
- show trends

Above all, the report emphasizes, data provide the substance for smart decisions. Informed decisions are ones that are considered and measured. They help us look thoroughly before we leap and, if we cannot resist the leaping, help us keep our bearings. Data stabilize our change efforts. Without data-based decision making, there is no rhyme nor reason to our change selection (Holly, 2003). Data help us avoid the wasteful, fruitless dissipation of resources indicated by the bubble map, they concentrate our minds and our resources— in order that we might have the greatest impact in areas of prioritized need. Educators work too hard to have their change efforts frittered away to nothing. They deserve better; they deserve to be able to use a process that works. They deserve a better path to school improvement.

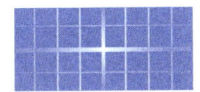

Creating a Data-Driven School Culture
Task 11: Reflecting on New Learning

Purpose: To reflect both individually and in Learning Teams about the professional impact of this workbook.

Grouping: Work individually and then meet with your Learning Team.

Directions: For the final pages of your reflective Change Log, working individually, respond to the following questions. When you have considered these questions and written your personal reflections, share your thoughts and ideas with your Learning Team colleagues.

As a result of reading the commentary and working on the tasks in this workbook, what are you going to do differently...

- as a classroom teacher?
- as a member of the Learning Team?
- as a member of the school faculty?
- as a member of the school district?

141

CHANGE LOG
Creating a Data-Driven School Culture

Notes

About the Author

Peter Holly is the author of the PATHWISE: *Data-Driven School Improvement Series*. Having been a teacher, administrator, researcher, and school improvement consultant in the United Kingdom, since 1990 he has worked solely with schools and school districts in the United States. He was one of the lead consultants for Schools for the Twenty-First Century in Washington State, the National Education Association's (NEA) Learning Lab project, and the New Iowa Schools initiative. Currently, he is an independent school improvement consultant working with school systems mainly in the Midwest. In helping school systems become more change-oriented and data-driven, he uses many of the materials to be found in this workbook.

References

American Association of School Administrators. (2002). *Using Data to Improve Schools: What's Working*. Arlington, VA: AASA.

Argyris, C. and Schon, D. (1978). *Organizational Learning: A Theory of Action Perspective*. Reading, Mass: Addison-Wesley.

Barth, R. (1991). *Improving Schools from Within*. San Francisco: Jossey-Bass.

Barth, R. (2002). *The Culture Builder*. Educational Leadership. May, 6-11.

Bellamy, G. Thomas, Holly, P., and Sinisi, R. (1997). *The Cycles of School Improvement*. National Staff Development Council.

Bernhardt, V. L. (1998). *Data Analysis for Comprehensive Schoolwide Improvement*. Larchmont, NY: Eye on Education.

Block, P. (1993). *Stewardship*. San Francisco: Berrett-Koehler.

Calhoun, E. (1994). *How to Use Action Research in the Self-Renewing School*. Alexandria, VA: Association for Supervision and Curriculum Development (ASCD).

Calhoun, E. (1999). *The Singular Power of One Goal*. Interview with Dennis Sparks. Journal of Staff Development; National Staff Development Council. Winter, 54-58.

Calhoun, E. (2002). *Action Research for School Improvement*. Educational Leadership. 59(6), 18-24.

Conner, D. (1995). *Managing at the Speed of Change*. Villard Books.

Conrath, J. (1986). *Our Other Youth*. Gig Harbor, WA.

Conzemius, A. (2000). *Framework: System Builds Change Efforts*. In Journal of Staff Development; National Staff Development Council. Winter, 21(1).

Covey, S. (1989). *Seven Habits of Highly Effective People*. New York: Simon and Schuster.

Csikszentmihalyi, M. (1990). *Flow: The Psychology of Optimal Experience*. New York: Harper-Collins.

Dolan, P. (1994). *Restructuring Our Schools*. Kansas City, MO: Systems and Organization.

Elmore, R. (1996). *Getting to Scale with Good Educational Practice*. Harvard Educational Review. Spring, 66(1).

Evans, J. (1996). *Three Stages of School Improvement*. Personal communication to the author.

Feddema, H. (1996). *Site-based Planning*. The Cambridge Group.

Festinger, L. (1954). *A Theory of Cognitive Dissonance*. Stanford, CA: Stanford.

REFERENCES

Forsythe, L. K. (1996). *The Transformation of Leadership through Quadrant Thinking: Fostering a Sense of Power for School Improvement*. In Issues facing Building Leaders Engaged in School Improvement (1997) Monograph Series. V11(2). Institute for Educational Leadership at the University of Northern Iowa.

Forsythe, L. K. (1999). *Reflections on Decision-Making*. Personal communication to the author.

Fullan, M. (1996). *Turning Systemic Thinking on Its Head*. Phi Delta Kappan. February, 420-423.

Gardner, J. (1963). *Self-Renewal*. New York: W.W. Norton.

Garmston, R. J. and Wellman, B. (1999). *The Adaptive School. A Sourcebook for Developing Collaborative Groups*. Norwood, MA: C. Gordon.

Garmston, R. J. (2002). *Group Wise*. Journal of Staff Development. 23(3), 74-75.

Gendlin, E.T. (1978). *Focusing*. New York: Everest House.

Glickman, C. (2001). *Dichotomizing Education: Why No One Wins and America Loses*. Phi Delta Kappan. October, 83(2), 147-152.

Goodlad, J. (1984). *A Place Called School*. New York: McGraw-Hill.

Guskey, T. (1990). *Integrating Innovations*. Educational Leadership. February, 11-15.

Hampel, R. (1995). *The Micropolitics of RE:Learning*. School Leadership. 5(6), November, 597-616.

Handy, C. (1984). *Taken for Granted? Understanding Schools as Organizations*. London: Longman/Schools Council.

Handy, C. (1989). *The Age of Unreason*. London: Heinemann.

Hatch, T. (2002). *When Improvement Programs Collide*. Phi Delta Kappan. 83(8), 626-635.

Hessel, K. and Holloway, J. (2002). *A Framework for School Leaders: Linking the ISLLC Standards to Practice*. Educational Testing Service (ETS).

Holcomb, E. L. (1999). *Getting Excited About Data: How to Combine People, Passion, and Proof*. Thousand Oaks, CA: Corwin Press.

Holly, P. (1990). *The Developing School*. Training Materials. National Education Association (NEA) Workshops.

Holly, P. (1995). *Why Essential Learnings?* Training Materials. New Iowa Schools Development Corporation (NISDC).

Holly, P. (1996). *Changing the Change Culture: The Three Stages of School Improvement*. Unpublished research paper.

REFERENCES

Holly, P. (1996). *Changing Trains*. Reflections Newsletter, New Iowa Schools Development Corporation (NISDC).

Holly, P. (1999). *Introducing Action Research*. Training Materials, The Learning Group.

Holly, P. (2000). *Data-Driven School Culture Survey*. The Learning Group.

Holly, P. (2003). *Creating a Data-Driven System*. In Educational Testing Service (ETS) forthcoming publication.

Holly, P. and Southworth, G. (1989). *The Developing School*. London: The Falmer Press.

Holly, P. and Lange, M. (2001). *Consultancy Report to Dubuque Schools*. The Learning Group.

Holly, P. and Lange, M. (2002). *Reflections on the Role of Data Coach*. The Learning Group.

Johnson, D.W. and Johnson, F.P. (2000). *Joining Together. Group Theory and Group Skills*. Boston: Allyn and Bacon.

Joyce, B. and Calhoun, E. (1995). *School Renewal: An Inquiry, not a Formula*. Educational Leadership, April.

Joyce, B., Wolf, J., and Calhoun, E. (1993). *The Self-Renewing School*. Alexandria, VA: ASCD.

Joyce, B., Showers, B., and Rolheiser-Bennett, C. (1987). *Staff Development and Student Learning: A Synthesis of Research on Models of Teaching*. Educational Leadership. 45(2).

Kanter, R. M. (1983). *The Change Masters*. New York: Simon and Schuster.

Lieberman, A. (1986). *Collaborative Research: Working With, Not Working On*. Educational Leadership, February.

Love, N. (2000). *Using Data — Getting Results*. Cambridge, MA: TERC.

McLaughlin, M. (1987). *Learning from Experience: Lessons from Policy Implementation*. Educational Evaluation and Policy Analysis. Summer, 9(2), 171-178.

Miller, E. (1996). *Idealists and Cynics: The Micropolitics of Systemic School Reform*. Harvard Education Letter. July/August, X11(4). Published by the Harvard Graduate School of Education.

Mintzberg, H. (1994). *The Fall and Rise of Strategic Planning*. Harvard Business Review, January-February.

Mitchell, J. (1990). Training Materials used with Dubuque Schools.

Noyce, P., Perda, D., and Traver, R. (2000). *Creating Data-Driven Schools*. Educational Leadership, February.

REFERENCES

Patterson, J.L., Purkey, S.C., and Parker, J.V. (1986). *Productive School Systems for a Non-Rational World.* Alexandria, VA: ASCD.

Peck, S. (1987). *The Different Drum: Community Making and Peace.* New York. Simon & Schuster.

Reys, R. (2001). *Curricular Controversy in the Math Wars: A Battle Without Winners.* Phi Delta Kappan. November, 83(3), 255-258.

Richardson, J. (1996). *If You Don't Know Where You're Going, How Will You Know When You Arrive?* School Team Innovator, September. NSCD.

Ries, A. (1996). *Focus. The Future of Your Company Depends On It.* New York: HarperCollins.

Sagor, R. (1993). *At-Risk Students: Reaching and Teaching Them.* Swampscott, Mass: Watersun Publishing Co.

Saphier, J., Bigda-Peyton, T., and Pierson, G. (1989). *How to Make Decisions that Stay Made.* Alexandria, VA: ASCD.

Schaefer, R. (1967). *The School as a Center of Inquiry.* New York: Harper and Row.

Schmoker, M. (1996). *Results: The Key to Continuous School Improvement.* Alexandria, VA: ASCD.

Schmoker, M. (2001). *The Results Fieldbook: Practical Strategies from Dramatically Improved Schools.* Alexandria, VA: ASCD.

Schon, D. (1971). *Beyond the Stable State.* London: Penguin Books.

Schon, D. (1983). *The Reflective Practitioner.* London: Temple Smith.

Senge, P. (1990). *The Fifth Discipline.* New York: Doubleday.

Timar, T. B. and Kirp, D. L. (1987). *Educational Reform and Institutional Competence.* Harvard Educational Review. 57(3), 308-330.

Tyack, D. (1999). *Endangered: Relentless Reform Threatens Schools that Already Work.* Education Week, December.

Tyack, D. and Cuban, L. (1999). *Tinkering toward Utopia: A Century of Public School Reform.* Boston: Harvard University Press.

Tyack, D. and Tobin, W. (1994). *The 'Grammar' of Schooling: Why has it been so hard to change?* American Educational Research Journal. Fall 31(3), 453-479.

Whitehead, A.N. (1932). *The Aims of Education.* London: Ernest Benn.

Appendix

Nancy Bradley, Director of School Improvement and Staff Development in Dubuque Community School District, Dubuque, Iowa, developed the following materials.

Dubuque Community School District (DCSD) Site Council Operational Checklist

> The main work of the DCSD Site Council is to develop, implement, monitor, and evaluate the Comprehensive School Improvement Plan (CSIP)

The Site Council will…

A. Gather input for development of the School Improvement Plan.

- ☐ *Input is solicited from various constituencies for development of the school's improvement targets (not just staff members).*

- ☐ *The Site Council keeps a proper perspective around the quantity of input (number of persons making any suggestion) as well as the quality of input.*

- ☐ *Efforts are made to broaden Site Council members' awareness of "best practices" in educational programming at this level (elementary, junior high, or high school) to enhance members' visionary scope and perspective of what "could be."*

- ☐ *The focus is kept on student achievement, not staff operation issues and concerns.*

- ☐ *The Site Council reviews the District Improvement Plan.*

APPENDIX

B. **Review and examine school data.**

☐ The creation and analysis of the School Profile begins the CSIP development process.

☐ This data informs the improvement goals/targets of the next CSIP.

☐ The School Profile...

☐ contains as much known data about the school as possible,

☐ represents a wide variety of information about the school in a concise format, and

☐ informs the Site Council on selection of future improvement targets for the school.

C. **Write the School Improvement Plan (or designate a group to write it based on the Council's established priorities).**

☐ The Site Council uses input from various constituencies and analysis from the School Profile to determine school improvement goals/targets for the next school year.

☐ The Site Council itself or a group named by the Site Council does the actual writing of the CSIP based on identified improvement targets.

☐ The Site Council reviews the CSIP yearly to see if the content is "too safe." Real school improvement moves beyond the safety zone and takes risks for students.

D. Create action teams to accomplish the goals of the School Improvement Plan.

- [ ] An action team exists for each school improvement goal/target.

- [ ] At the beginning of the school year each action team needs to ...

    - [ ] have identified members,

    - [ ] know its essential work as defined by the Site Council,

    - [ ] have identified times to meet regularly throughout the year,

    - [ ] know its success indicators upon which its progress will be measured and reported,

    - [ ] know what data it will collect for progress evaluation in the identified work area(s), and

    - [ ] collect baseline data at the beginning of the year and final progress data at the end of the year to provide feedback to the Site Council on its progress in the areas of success indicators.

- [ ] The Site Council sees that the resources needed by each action team are provided (e.g., time, funding, information).

APPENDIX

E. Have action teams report progress to the Site Council, which supports and encourages, gives feedback on action plans and on the work of the action team, and works with collected assessment data.

- [ ] Each action team reports its progress in its success indicator areas at least two times per year (three or four may be more desirable).

- [ ] The Site Council regularly reviews the work in progress of each action team in its identified work area, giving support and encouragement, providing feedback, and asking "critical friend" questions when necessary to re-focus and/or set expectations for the action team.

- [ ] The Site Council makes certain that the work of each action team is known by all other action teams and the entire faculty/staff for purposes of information and collaboration.

- [ ] The Site Council monitors action teams' collected assessment data throughout the year.

- [ ] The Site Council uses end-of-year assessment data to provide summary and evaluation information to the Superintendent of Schools as well as to inform the next year's CSIP.

Other operational structures for the Site Council to keep in mind:

- [ ] Site Council by-laws are reviewed at least every three years to consider possible need for revision/amendment.

☐ A principal's operations ("nuts & bolts") committee and/or structure is identified and functional to keep daily operation issues from taking the time and attention of the Site Council away from its visionary work.

☐ Operational Norms

  ☐ Site Council members have discussed and identified a few collectively agreed upon guidelines for the effective operation of the Site Council.

  ☐ Operational norms are reviewed and revised with every membership change on the Site Council.

  ☐ Operational norms are posted or distributed at each Site Council meeting.

☐ The Site Council meets regularly and as often as necessary to conduct its business effectively.

☐ Minutes

  ☐ Minutes of each Site Council meeting are taken and posted/disseminated within 24-48 hours of the meeting.

  ☐ The work of the Site Council/CSIP is regularly published in a condensed form and in the principal's newsletter to parents.

☐ Permanent Site Council archives are maintained in the school office by year and include each year's agenda, minutes, and CSIP.

APPENDIX

- [ ] Membership

  - [ ] Each member on the Site Council represents a defined constituency.

  - [ ] A rotation is established for Site Council membership for a yearly change of members that is not disproportionately high for any membership group.

  - [ ] Members have regular feedback/input connections with their constituency.

  - [ ] All groups represented have equal voice.

  - [ ] Staff members and non-staff members should be approximately equal in number; Site Council membership should not be dominated by any particular group.

  - [ ] The PTA/PTO/PTC/Booster Club president or designated representative should be a member of the Site Council.

- [ ] Roles needed for Site Council operation are clearly defined and assigned:

  - [ ] Facilitator–conducts meetings

  - [ ] Chairperson (usually the principal)–is responsible for the preparation of the agenda with the facilitator

  - [ ] Recorder–takes minutes at each meeting and distributes them within 24–48 hours of the meeting

  - [ ] Evaluator–ends the meeting with process feedback to the Site Council on how well it conducted its work at the meeting (e.g., time, focus, discussion, adherence to operational norms)

APPENDIX

School: _____
Comprehensive School Improvement Plan
School Year: _____

Action Team Yearly Plan

■ Action Team _____

■ Action Team Members *(please note chairperson)*

■ Forum Site Council liaison _____

■ District goal area (Please check)
- ☐ Reading
- ☐ Mathematics
- ☐ Other Instructional Programs
- ☐ Respect, Citizenship, Character
- ☐ Communication and Collaboration

■ School's goal(s) related to this Action Team

APPENDIX

■ What is/are the purpose(s)/essential work of your Action Team?

■ What results do you expect by this June?

■ What is your team's action plan for school year: _____? (How will you accomplish your team's essential work?)

Activity   **Timeline**

■ What will be your Action Team's indicators of its success this year?

APPENDIX

- What data and evaluative information will you gather and report to the Site Council to represent the progress towards your Action Team's goal(s) this school year? *(Please include the nature of the baseline, up-close, and trend-line data from which your team will measure and report its end-of-the-year progress data.)*

- Will your team need staff development this year? If so, please describe.

- What questions/requests do you have for the Site Council in its supportive role to Action Teams?

APPENDIX

Comprehensive School Improvement Plan
School Year: _____

Action Team Quarterly Update to the Site Council

Action Team: _____

Chairperson: _____

Reporting Period: _____

> Report Due Dates:
> - November ___
> - January ___
> - April ___
> - May ___
> - End-of-Year Summary and Evaluation
>
> *Please submit each update to the Site Council on or before the due date.*

■ What has been the focus and what were the related activities of this action team during this time period?

■ What has been accomplished during this quarter?

Implementation of _____ School Plan

The following provides a listing of expectations and tasks that are necessary to execute the _____ School Plan.

Administration will:

- Establish action teams based on the school plan and staff members' interests
- Share the building plan with the entire staff, Site Council, and other interested groups at the beginning of the school year
- Support and facilitate activities of the action teams

Action Teams will:

- Develop a yearly calendar of activities
- Meet on a regular basis
- Gather baseline data for their goal area
- Provide trimester updates to the Site Council
- Develop a summary sheet based on Success Criteria
- Interpret data and make suggestions at faculty meetings
- Review with staff the steps needed to reach the goal (Supporting Activities)

Action Team Chairperson will:

- Meet on a regular basis with the principal to plan and share progress
- Summarize and assess progress on the school plan
- Review the building plan based on input from the action team

Notes

Notes

Notes

Notes

These materials are being sponsored by the Teaching and Learning Division of Educational Testing Service (ETS), a not for profit organization. One of the division's goals is to serve teachers' professional development needs by providing products and services that identify, assess, and advance good teaching from initial preparation through advanced practice.

ETS Educational Testing Service
Teaching and Learning Division

Our mission is to help advance quality and equity in education by providing fair and valid assessments, research and related services. Our products and services measure knowledge and skills, promote learning and performance, and support education and professional development for all people worldwide.

We welcome your comments and feedback.

Email address: professionaldevelopment@ets.org

Professional Development Group
Teaching and Learning Division
Educational Testing Service, MS 18-D
Princeton, New Jersey 08541